A PATH TO ORIENTAL WISDOM
Introductory Studies in Eastern Philosophy

Sumi-e illustrations and photos by
Carolyn Parulski

A PATH TO ORIENTAL WISDOM

Introductory Studies in Eastern Philosophy

by
George Parulski, Jr.

EDITED BY CHARLES LUCAS

GRAPHIC DESIGN BY DAVID PAUL KAPLAN

©Ohara Publications, Incorporated 1976
Printed in the United States of America
Library of Congress Catalog Card Number: 76-21011

Seventh Printing 1986

ISBN 0-89750-046-6

OHARA ⬚ PUBLICATIONS, INCORPORATED

BURBANK, CALIFORNIA

DEDICATION

Works of philosophy are produced in time, in history by existent philosophers who are at the mercy of their own experience; philosophers who live on the threshold of experience and also at its outer limits. They have tentacles that search in the nooks and crannies, and truth for them is usually purchased at a great price. The vision of the philosopher is their all, and they attempt to shine this vision as a light on the darkness of experience to enlighten experience (and also to make it light). They tell us who we are and what we are; they show us ourselves. To all these men and women this book is sincerely dedicated.

and

To my wife, Carolyn, who made this text a reality.

ACKNOWLEDGEMENTS

I wish to express my sincere thanks to Zen Master Kuzure Kudo who helped me in the translation of the Oriental texts. To Zen Master Pakuin, Director of the Eisho-ji Zen Temple, who read over all the translations for accuracy. Finally I wish to express my thanks to Carolyn Parulski who donated time and effort in producing original sumi-e illustrations.

Introduction

There is no such thing as a "Bible of Oriental Philosophy" in the sense of an authoritative statement of the teachings of Oriental Philosophy, and for this there are two reasons. First, because the Oriental Philosophies recognize no authority, human or divine; and secondly, because the range of beliefs, language, countries and time involved, would make such a volume impossible to compile.

The bulk of knowledge of Oriental Philosophy is held within the actual sermons, allegedly given by the various founders and minor commentaries written by the many followers.

There are few Scriptures actually written by the respected founders but they seem to have later been compiled by followers. The commentaries I have spoken of are considered of lesser importance compared to the Scriptures, and were written by people who lived their respective systems.

Our Western knowledge of the Scriptures is not yet a hundred years old. First came sporadic translations of odd Scriptures; then, a mere seventy years ago, Max Muller's *Sacred Books of the East* gave Western minds an inkling of the treasures awaiting them. Anthologies from corners of the Oriental Philosophy field appeared from time to time, ranging from Beal's *Catena of Scriptures from the Chinese* (1871) to Warren's *Buddhism in Translations* (1906) from the Pali Canon of the Theravada School of Ceylon.

The first attempt at an anthology drawn from the whole field was only made in 1938, in the second edition of Dwight Goddard's *A Buddhist Bible*, but the versions there given are far too free to be worthy of their subject. Then came Clareto Hamilton's *Buddhism, A Religion of Infinite Compassion* (New York, 1952), chosen primarily for college students; but the best anthology to date of any Scriptures is *Oriental Philosophy Texts*

Through the Ages, published in London in 1954, and edited by Dr. Edward Conze, composed of translations from original languages by a team of experts, Miss I.B. Horner for Pali (Hinayana), Dr. Conze for Indian Mahayana, Dr. David Snellgrove for Tibet and Dr. Arthur Waley for China and Japan.

The one thing all these books have in common is that they are aimed at the person with previous knowledge in the field or with some type of scholarly knowledge. The average layman picking up these books would find them impossible to comprehend.

The need for a book written in simple, clear-cut language has been necessary for many years.

This volume allots the right proportions of space to the various schools in the vast field of Oriental Philosophy. There is a brief explanation of Taoism and Confucianism; a complete examination of the Buddhist Philosophy and a look at the Hindu Philosophies, some of which have never been explained in the English language. The major portion of the text is of the wisdom of the Orientals. Thus, we can see that the first three parts are meant to bring the readers understanding of the field far enough to enjoy and grow with the pieces of wisdom, selected from over 75 different sources.

Having been in the field of Oriental Philosophy for fifty years of my life, I find this text both refreshing and a necessary addition to its field.

ROSHI PAKUIN
Director
Eisho-ji Zen Temple
Corning, New York

October, 1975

Author's Introduction

"The nightingale sings its song
but alas, no one listens,
Why, nightingale?
Oh, why?"

The Orient has always been considered a source of both mystery and awe. Their cultures span thousands of years of rich colorful heritage. Included in this heritage are their philosophies.

One need not be a scholar to enjoy the thoughts and principles the greatest of philosophers have laid down for us. For in true definition, philosophy is none other than the love, study and pursuit of wisdom or knowledge of things and their causes, be it theoretical or practical. With this definition in mind, anyone of us can be considered philosophers. We are all in the pursuit of knowledge of ourselves and our environment since the day we first opened our eyes. From the first time we asked "Why?," we have tried to understand the making of things. How often have you said, "Well, you have your philosophy and I have mine"? What we have said in this context is that each has his own thought pattern, thus a philosophy of his own.

It is the sin of existence when man, no longer in search of knowledge, stops asking that simple question, "Why?" Yet when in life are we ever really sure of anything? It is our ignorance and fear of losing this mental security that tells our minds to stop!

So we go on, afraid to ask the questions of life. This then is the difference between the philosopher and the nonphilosopher. A philosopher will ask again the whys and will continue, never satisfied, in his quest for understanding the nature of things. While the nonphilosopher, because of his fear and/or ignorance, will hold back and never really become at peace with himself.

Perhaps this is what the philsopher is: a person who is curious. A person who wants to intensify his life by plunging deeply into the nature of things, to answer for himself the basic riddles that still puzzle mankind.

So why will this person go on all the days of life thinking about this or that riddle? No other reason than to gain peace with himself, for when there are no unseen questions and thoughts for answers there can be no unknown. Without an unknown there is little fear, but instead peacefulness and true security.

To sum up the purpose of philosophy in one word, we can say that philosophy is to "intensify" life, to make it fuller and happier.

If it is the purpose of a philosopher to be happy, then we can all be philosophers. Philosophy is not just something for the elite intellectual, but for all people to live and grow by.

To make life happier and to explain the nature of things are the two major purposes in the creation of Oriental Philosophy. To try to narrow all the Oriental Philosophies to one interpretation would be impossible, for each has a different means to the same end. Therefore, each system approaches the riddle of existence differently, but each arrives at the same answer.

The Oriental Philosophers, in general, are nature oriented. By this I mean that they pattern themselves after the laws of nature. Man is a natural organism and in order for him to gain harmony with the universe and achieve total happiness, he must follow the ways nature has set for him. Most Oriental Philosophers agree that the universe is the only thing in creation that is permanent; all parts within the universe are subject to constant change. It can be compared to an engine. The engine itself is the only thing that does not change. All the parts within are subject to constant change, yet the basic law of movement is fixed.

So, too, the universe is the engine. Nature, man and life are moving parts that are constantly changing. Yet there is a general order to this change; it is not blind movement.

To look at this once again, the Oriental Philosophers are "nature oriented" in that the laws of nature are the laws a person follows to gain harmony within himself. When the person is at peace with himself and all around him, the change becomes a natural thing and the person is uplifted from the bonds of everyday life and becomes one with the universe. This way, when the wind blows, the man is also in movement, not in the scientific sense, but he can feel and experience the wind's movement, as if he and the wind were one. He becomes empathic towards all life and being thus intensifies the senses.

All this is achieved when the mental outlook of the philosopher is geared towards the right path. The essays that follow will help the reader to understand the underlying principles of the Oriental Philosophies and help him place the proper foot on the path of understanding the Inner Self.

Preface

Overviews of philosophical systems are frequently fraught with omissions or distortions that waylay serious inquiry and take the reader down paths to nowhere. Oriental philosophy is particularly vulnerable to one-sided presentations that create more misconceptions than understanding.

The present work is refreshing in its balanced perspective. It does not present the mere details of Eastern thought, but rather provides the reader with the spirit of these ideas.

This book does not obscure the reader's view with unnecessary foliage, but rather presents him with a sturdy trunk which can be developed with further cultivation. Its expressed purpose is to reach the average reader. The pace is slow so that the reader can enjoy the scenery, yet it appeals to the more knowledgeable.

Euro-Americans are prone to view Eastern thought as the antithesis of Western philosophy. This notion is based on the assumption that Eastern thought is essentially homogenous. The fallacy of this assertion is easily seen after reading this book, as the profound range of differences presented here underscores the magnitude of human variation.

Others have treated the topics discussed here as religions, and have argued that only in the West have true philosophical systems developed. This is a restrictive definition of philosophy.

The study of these Oriental concepts can do much to promote the development of new perspectives on traditional Western philosophies.

Never has an understanding of Eastern thought been more important. With such problems as world famine and nuclear holocaust dangling over our heads, man's search for the meaning has never seemed more relevant. Concomitant with what appears to be the increased probability of man's annihilation has been a turning inward to search for meaning. For centuries, Hinduism and Buddhism have illuminated man's reason for existence. These ancient epistemologies are as valid for this age as for any previous. Presented in this book are the basics for a firm understanding of these profound ideas.

THOMAS PRICE
December, 1975

Contents

Part One
Taoist and Confucian Philosophy

"The Sage-like man knows the way of
what the ancients called The Heavenly
Treasure House. He may pour into it
without its being filled up; he may pour
from it without its being exhausted; and
all this time he does not know from
whence the supply comes."

—CHUANG-TSE

CHAPTER ONE

"The Way of Life"

The first and most mystical of the Oriental Philosophies discussed is Taoism.

Taoism is said to have been originated in the Sixth Century B.C. by the great philosopher Lao-tse.

Lao-tse was said to have been born in the village of Keuh-jin, in the parish of Le, in the district of Tsou, where he was called Li-peh Yang.

We know little of Li's younger days and sometimes the question arises if Li ever really existed.

Those who think Taoism was originated by Lao-tse generally believe him to have been the Keeper of the Royal Archives in Lo-yang, the capital city in that time period. His working in the Royal Archives gave Li the opportunity to study the great scriptures of that era.

Li's fame grew and soon he was known as Lao-tse, which translates as the "Old Philosopher." But with or without fame, Lao-tse remained the Keeper of the Royal Archives.

As time went on his ruler became greedy and selfish with power. This hurt the old man and he decided to leave the place he had known all his life; leave the province he had sprung from to seek a better way.

As he passed the border of the city limits he was interrupted by its guardian who recognized the old man as being the great philosopher and said to him, "You are a great man. Why is it you have never committed your genius to paper?"

Lao-tse, understanding the situation, wrote down his beliefs and philosophies in 81 verses of poetry. He called this little book the *Tao-Te-Ching*, which translates as the *Book of Virtue and Reason*.

Lao-tse left and was never heard from again.

This book, although only 81 pages, covers more concepts and ideas than many encyclopedias. The heart and soul of Taoism is embodied in that small text. Many interpretations of the *Tao-Te-Ching* have been written in the length of thousands of pages, but none explains it better than the work itself. Perhaps a deeper look into the concept of the Tao might clarify this.

The Tao translates as the "way," "path," "road" or the "light that shines in the darkness for all to follow." The Tao is the topic of the *Tao-Te-Ching* and the principle force underlying Taoism.

There are three kinds of Tao or manifestations of the Tao.

The first is the Tao of the Ultimate Reality. This Tao cannot be revealed for it shines too brightly for the human eye to see. No mortal can uphold its vision, its magnificent brightness. Through this Tao all came to be known as it is today. All started under it and all will perish under it. This Tao is the Way of Wisdom, the giver of Spiritual Essence, of form (hsuang).

The second manifestation of the Tao is the Tao of the Universe. This Tao sets the way for all mankind to act. It is the ordering force to all of nature and all we call reality. It is the norm of existence, the rhythm of life. When the Tao is in this form it enters and "assumes life." It gives us love and meaning.

The third manifestation of the Tao is the Way we should order our lives. It is a system of ethics, theories for good and bad. It gives us a means to judge what is moral or immoral. It tells us what to do to be true to ourselves and our chosen system of society. Finally it helps us gear in with the way the universe operates.

The "Te" of the *Tao-Te-Ching* translates as "reason," "virtue" or "power." If we use this translation of power we can see it in three forms, the same as we observed the Tao in three forms. There are the powers of magic, mystery and philosophy.

The power of Magic became the Popular Taoism or that which was followed by the masses. This Taoism was able to be grasped by the ordinary person and not just the intellectual. Taoism in general and the *Tao-Te-Ching* were thought to be aimed at the intellect of the scholar. Popular Taoism was able to be understood by all and therefore gained a great deal of appeal. Yet this type of Taoism was not a pretty sight. It prostituted the high order of the *Tao-Te-Ching* and turned it into something perverse. It turned a "guide" into a stagnant pond. Mysticism became mystification and religion perverted into necromancy and sorcery.

The second power of the universe is Mystical. This can be seen in what is called Esoteric Taoism. This Taoism incorporated alchemy and magic (superstition) in its form. These followers believed that the *Tao-Te-Ching* was a book of spells, the way to find the Tao and was their source of mystical power.

Instead of self-seeking (as in Common Taoism) they centered around purification. Their bodies were considered temples and had to be purified so the power of the Tao would pass through them and assume their being, thus granting them magical powers. This purification was a ritual that comprised many steps. The major steps were:

—Placing the body in yogic-like postures (see Chapter Eight)

—Performing abdominal breathing

—Chanting the poems of the *Tao-Te-Ching*.

This exercise helps to unite the mind and body. When the mind and body are united, the person is one with himself and one with the universe.

At the completion of years of these exercises, the body became pliable and therefore adaptable for the mysterious flow of Tao.

Some thought this Tao was capable of granting immortality. Chang-tao-ling was an advocate of this belief and held to the reasoning that there was an island somewhere near the South Pole where the mysterious River of Eternal Life flowed. But only if the body was purified through the three steps, and the ideals of the *Tao-Te-Ching* held, could eternal life be granted. Since it is almost humanly impossible for a being to be as perfect as the *Tao-Te-Ching* commands, no one to date has ever been granted immortality. That is not to say they aren't still trying. The descendant of Chang-tao-ling is called the Pearly Emperor and lives on the Dragon-Tiger Mountain near Kiang-si. He rules his followers to this day with the power of a king.

The third manifestation of power is Philosophical. This power will only enter the life of someone who is reflective and has intuitively geared himself in the way of the universe.

Of the three, Esoteric Taoism is near extinction, Popular Taoism is corrupt and Philosophical Taoism is alive and well and still shaping the lives of the Chinese people.

CHAPTER TWO

"The Great Teacher"

Confucianism was founded in the Sixth Century by Ch'iu K'ung (551—479 B.C.), son of Shuh-liang Heih, governor of Tsow.

When Shuh-liang Heih died he left his wife very poor, but she managed enough to raise a son, young Ch'iu, and reared him with a good education. His teachers praised the youth for his extraordinary intelligence and many came to listen to the young man talk.

At the age of nineteen he married and was given the position of Keeper of the Granaries.

Even at this young age he made many improvements in the education and administration of the Tsow district. This impressed the minister and he promoted young Ch'iu to the position of Superintendent of the Fields. It was a high position for someone in his twenties.

Although the youth was under great stress and had little time to himself, he managed to read many sources of music, history and his favorite, poetry.

His fame and knowledge grew and soon all came to know him as a great scholar. People called him K'ung-fu Tse, which translates as "K'ung the Philosopher."

Confucius authored five classics. There are an additional four books that comprise the Confucian belief.

The Five Classics are:

—The *I-Ching* or the *Book of Changes*
—The *Shu Ching* or the *Book of Poetry*
—The *Shih Ching* or the *Book of History*
—The *Li Chi* or the *Book of Ceremonies and Rites*, and
—The *Ch'un Ch'iu* or the *Spring and Autumn Annals.*

Only the *Ch'un Ch'iu* was written entirely by Confucius and is basically a history text. The others are said to have either been edited by him or compiled by later followers.

The Four Books are:

—The *Lun Yu* or the *Analects*
—The *Ta Hsueh* or the *Great Learning*
—The *Chung Yung* or the *Doctrine of the Mean*
—The *Meng-tse Shu* or the *Book of Mencius.*

The *I-Ching* is undoubtedly very ancient and dates from earlier Chou times. The *I-Ching* is unquestionably one of the most important books in world literature. It was one of the few books that escaped the great book burnings of Chin Shih Huang Ti (213 B.C.). Huang Ti was an advocate of Buddhism and being in a high government position decided to burn all books that did not relate to Buddhism, except those of Taoism and the *I-Ching* (he believed in Chang-tao-ling and his claims of eternal life).

The *I-Ching* is a collection of 64 six-line symbols or oracles referred to as hexagrams (hexa meaning six; grams referring to lines). These hexagrams are made up of two three-line oracles called trigrams (tri=three) or in Chinese, pa-kua.

The oracles themselves are composed of an arrangement of straight (——) and broken (— —) lines.

In days gone by, oracles were used only with one line, the straight representing yes, and the broken representing no.

But as time went on, the need for differentiation seemed to have been felt. It was at this time the single lines were coupled into pairs:

Later a third line was added. These trigrams were conceived as images and attributes of all that goes on in heaven and on earth. They were held to be in constant change, one trigram easily changed into another. This is the fundamental concept of the *Book of Changes*. All the oracles are in a state of change, their image connotes this as does their meaning.

The pa-kuas represent a family in the abstract sense. The family consists of a father (☰) and a mother (☷), an oldest son (☳), second son (☵), youngest son (☶), and oldest daughter (☴), second daughter (☲) and a youngest daughter (☱). The sons represent the principles of movement in various stages—beginning of movement, resting in movement and danger in movement. The daughters represent devotion in all its stages, that is—gentle penetration, clarity and adaptability and joyous tranquility.

The major figures in the history of the *I-Ching* are: Fu Hsi, King Wan, the Duke of Chou and Confucius.

Fu Hsi belonged to the period of the Five Kings (2852—2205 B.C.). It is said that one day while he was hunting he came across a turtle returning to his home in the lake. He observed the patterns on its shell. They were an unusual arrangement of three lines, some broken, others unbroken. With much meditation, Fu Hsi is said to have patterned a system of wisdom and divination from these lines.

The first book of the *Book of Changes* appeared in the Hsia dynasty (2205—1766 B.C.) under the title *Lien Shan*. The second edition of this text appeared during the Shang dynasty (1766—1150 B.C.) under the title *Kuei Ts'uang*.

It was during this time the *I-Ching* was thought of as only a book of divination. Each situation demanded the action proper to it. In every situation, there is a right and wrong course of action. The right brings good fortune, the wrong misfortune. Which then is the right *course* in a given situation? This question was the decisive factor. As a result, the *I-Ching* was lifted from the job of being merely for divination. If a fortune teller, on reading her cards, tells her client that he hasn't long to wait for his new house, there is nothing for the client to do except wait for the house to come—or not to come. What then is foretold is mere fate; the individual has no say in its action. For this reason, fortune telling lacked moral significance. When it happened in China that the client did not just sit and wait for fate, instead asking, "What am I to do?", the *I-Ching* had to be more than a book of divination; it had also to be a book of wisdom.

It was due to King Wan (1150 B.C.) and his son the Duke of Chou, that the *I-Ching* became a book of wisdom. With each hexagram they wrote commentaries on its meaning.

It was in this state that the *I-Ching* fell into the hands of Confucius. Confucius modified the text by arranging each hexagram in a logical order. He also wrote commentaries about each line in each and every hexagram. Therefore, a straight line in one hexagram differed in meaning from a straight line in another.

Among the followers of Confucius was a man named Pu Shang

(Tze Hsia) who spread the knowledge of the *I-Ching* throughout China. He also incorporated the philosophy of the *Doctrine of the Mean* and the *Great Learning* in the text.

It was during the Han dynasty (1662—1722 A.D.) that K'ang Hsi organized the philosophical commentaries of Pu Shang and the text of Confucius and made a translation that most *I-Ching* scholars use today.

The *I-Ching* has three basic principles. The first is change. Confucius said in the *Analects*, "Everything flows on and on like this river, without pause day and night."

The river is flowing and constantly under change. If you stand on the shoreline of the river one day, the next day when you return the shoreline is not the same. There are different deposits of soils, shells, maybe even the color of the water. In all reality the shore is NOT the same shore that rested near the river yesterday. Yet the river does not change.

Confucius said, "Nature is always in motion, always changing, therefore to remain within life's forces, you must always be in motion, always changing."

The second principle of the *I-Ching* is ideas. It is believed that all reality in this world is only the appearance of something existing in another world, a world of ideas.

Every event is only an action that has happened before in another world beyond our sense perception. It is from this world that the *I-Ching* draws its knowledge of things to happen, for to the *I-Ching* they have already happened. Thus, the *I-Ching* relates only history.

The third principle of the *I-Ching* is judgment. The judgments clothe the images of the words, as it were; they indicate whether a given action will bring good fortune or bad, remorse or humiliation. The judgments make it possible for a man to make a decision to desist from a course of action indicated by the situation of the moment that might turn out harmful in the long run. In this way he makes himself independent from the flow of events.

The trigrams that were originally ordered by Fu Hsi looked like this:

The trigrams as defined by King Wan look like this:

	NAME	ATTRIBUTES	SYMBOLS
☰	Chien (creative)	Strong	Heaven
☷	K'un (receptive)	Devoted Yielding	Earth
☳	Chen (arousing)	Inciting movement	Thunder
☵	Kan (abysmal)	Dangerous	Water
☶	Ken (keeping still)	Resting	Mountain
☴	Sun (gentle)	Penetrating	Wind Wood
☲	Li (light-giving)	Clinging	Fire
☱	Tui (joyful)	Joyful	Lake

When two of these trigrams are put together they become hexagrams. These are the hexagrams:

	Khien	Symbol of male firmness. In nature it is the heavens. In the family, the father; in society, the king.
	K'un	Symbol for submission. In nature it is earth. In the family it is the mother; in society, the people.
	Mang	Symbol of obscurity. Shows experience in youth.
	Hsu	Symbol of waiting. Delay.

䷅	Sung	Symbol of contention. Confliction in sight.
䷂	Chun	Symbol of bursting. Difficulties in starting off.
䷆	Sze	Symbol of multitude. Group action in near sight.
䷇	Pi	Symbol of collaboration. Union with the forces of good.
䷊	Thai	Symbol of success. Peace and progress sings in the air.
䷋	Phi	Symbol of failure. Stagnation smells in low movement breeze.
䷌	Thung Zan	Symbol of community. Companionship is the father of happiness.
䷍	Ta Yu	Symbol of abundance. The season is full of grace and all possess much.
䷎	Ch'ien	Symbol of humility. A wise man walks with his head bowed.
䷏	Yu	Symbol of harmony. A sign of goodness is enthusiasm for tomorrow.

CONTINUED

Sui	Symbol of succession. It is better to follow, than never to be involved at all.
Ku	The symbol of major power. The bird will not fly, for it has been stripped of its wings.
Lin	Symbol of advance. Father, I can touch the stars.
Kwan	Symbol of contemplation. Before you cross the bridge, look first to see if it is there.
Shih Ho	Symbol of criminal proceedings.
Pi	Symbol of model. The moon is the ornament of the heavens.
Po	Symbol of dispersion. Collapse, falling apart.
Fu	Symbol of reversal. When beauty is known as beauty, ugliness is there.
Wu Wang	Symbol of innocence. To be free from error.
Ta Khu	Symbol of great taming force. When you are one with the universe, you are one with all animals.

☷ I		Symbol of sustenance. Nourishment.
☱ Ta Kwo		Symbol of major preponderance. Large in excess.
☵ Khan		Symbol of sinking. Abysmal.
☲ Li		Symbol of adherence, fire and light. The light clings to the sun, the shadow to the stars.
☱ Hsien		Symbol of mutual influence. I cry because you are not here.
☳ Hang		Symbol of perseverance. The road is long and hard, but a journey begins and ends with but one step.
☰ Thun		Symbol of regression. Is better to step back than to lose the foot.
☳ Ta Kwang		Symbol of major power. Great strength.
☷ Chin		Symbol of progress. If you try hard enough, you will succeed.
☷ Ming		Symbol of lack of appreciation. The light has darkened.

CONTINUED

☷	Kia Zan	Symbol of the family. Your greatest friend is your family.
☷	Khwei	Symbol of opposition.
☷	Kien	Symbol of difficulty.
☷	Chien	Symbol of deliverance.
☷	Sun	Symbol of diminution. Decrease.
☷	Yi	Symbol of addition. A family of two soon becomes three.
☷	Kwai	Symbol of resoluteness. To break through.
☷	Kuo	You are one. Symbol of coming to meet. Intercourse.
☷	Ts'ui	Symbol of collection. In the market place many gather together.
☷	Shang	Symbol of pushing upward. The goal is light, and I hold it in my hands.

☷ Khwan	Symbol of repression.	
☵ Ching	Symbol of source. The noise from the well speaks the truth.	
☱ Ko	Symbol of change. Revolution.	
☲ Ting	Symbol of nourishment. The cauldron is misty.	
☶ Kan	The symbol of exciting power. As I join in love, heaven is at my feet.	
☳ Kien	Symbol of gradual progress. Nothing comes easy.	
☴ Kwei Mei	Symbol of marriage. Oh, marrying maiden, show me your hand, so I may become golden.	
☵ Fang	Symbol of prosperity.	
☶ Lu	Symbol of wandering. A stranger has just arrived.	
☴ Sun	Symbol of penetrating. Wind and wood.	

CONTINUED

CONTINUED

☱ Tui		The symbol of pleasure. From my boat I see the water on the lake, the light in the sky and me in myself.
☵ Hwan		Symbol of dispersion. Dissolution.
☱ Kieh		Symbol of regulated restriction. Even the sky has limits.
☴ Chung Fu		Symbol of truth. Better to be impolite than tell a lie.
☳ Hsiao Kwo		Symbol of minor preponderance. Small excess.
☵ Chi Chi		Symbol of accomplishment. Remove your shoes and rest, you are there.
☲ Wei Chi		Symbol of what is yet not accomplished.
☶ Ken		Symbol of stability. Keeping still.
☴ Hsiao Khu		Symbol of taming force. To restrain something, in minor case.
☲ Lu		A time for deliberate action. Treat carefully.

The *I-Ching* is consulted by the casting of yarrow sticks which usually comprises a long ritual. Centuries passed before the shorter method of using Chinese coins (bronze) was adopted. Today, three pennies may be substituted for the Chinese coins. The line drawn will depend on the face which appears. For example, if using pennies, three heads equal a broken line, three tails a solid line, two heads and one tail a solid line and two tails and one head equal a broken line.

After the lines are arranged (first line is drawn on the bottom working up), you consult the text for the interpretation.

The *Shu Ching*, which translates as the *Book of History*, is also a great work dating from the Chou Period. Its range is from about 2400 B.C. to 750 B.C. It is a collection of historical documents and proclamations; a formulation of political ideas and fundamentals of good government.

The *Shih Ching* is a collection of 305 best poems (reputedly from a collection of 3,000 poems written during several preceding centuries). The book stresses the cherishing of thoughts and sentiments of your forebears. Some of the poems are odes written for various occasions. Some of the poems are lyrical. This book is a valuable insight into the manner and customs of ancient China.

The *Li Chi* is the book of *Ceremonies and Rites*. It is a voluminous work on etiquette. It was edited about 100 B.C. by the two Tai cousins, and it is based on documents allegedly written by Confucius.

The *Ch'un Ch'iu* or the *Spring and Autumn Annals*, is a history of Confucius' province of Lu from 722 to 484 B.C. It was called the *Spring and Autumn Annals* by its readers who said, "Its praises are as stimulating as spring, while its censures are as withering as autumn."

The *Analects* (*Lun Yu*) were compiled c. 450—375 B.C. They make a book of twenty-four chapters, composed of sayings of Confucius collected by his followers. This book gives us the best conception of Confucius and Confucianism that we have.

The *Great Learning* represents Confucius' ideas of the Superior Man, the ideal each of us should strive for.

The *Doctrine of the Mean* shows that if you are a Superior Man you can only produce harmony between heaven, earth and man. You can do no evil.

One hundred years after the death of Confucius, Mencius (or Meng-tse, translated as Meng the Philosopher) was born. He too, valued the ideals of Confucius and soon became famous for his wisdom.

Mencius believed that all human nature was good and what evil there is in man is learned. Mencius supported this conception by saying that there are no evil or bad qualities in the human form at birth; therefore, evil is learned through one's life experience.

Mencius believed in morals that he called the "Five Constant Virtues." They are:

—BENEVOLENCE: to work for the good of the people

—RIGHTEOUSNESS: do unto others as you would have them do unto you

—PROPRIETY: treating people with kindness and justice

—WISDOM: let knowledge be your goal. The greatest form of good is knowledge; the lack of it is ignorance. Mencius told his followers, "Look upward to wisdom, never seeking other desires"

—SINCERITY: be sincere in all you do. Without sincerity the world cannot exist.

Opposite Mencius' views were those of Hsun-tse (320—235 B.C.?). He believed that all men are evil and that good is learned. He advocated living with people who have *learned* good so this good will rub off on you. In turn, Mencius advocated living separately from society so the good will remain with you. Hsun-tse believed in practicing a form of quiet meditation (similar to the Esoteric Taoist meditation). With this meditation true wisdom is gained.

While Taoism taught knowledge (Tao) through either Philosophy, Magic (Popular) or Quietistic Meditation (Esoteric), what held Confucianism through the centuries? What qualities did this system teach?

There are five views that a person should keep as his morals. These concepts, when made pertinent to your being, will help you fit into society. These bright values are timeless in that they will help you fit into the norms of any society at any point in time. They are goals of personal character and social life.

These five views are:

The first concept is called "Jen." Jen means, in translation, MAN. It pertains to the relationship between man and man. This can be defined as love, benevolence and compassion. This relationship was to transcend the perfection of nature and become oneness with all. This *all* referring to the relationship between man and man.

This man-and-man relationship would transcend even the boundaries of death. "It is better to accept death than break the relationship of Jen."

Confucius held this virtue of relationship as being the most important level to reach in a lifetime. He said, "Man-and-man is the most important because it is man we live with and it is man we are to love."

The second concept is called Chu-tse or the "Superior Man." It refers to the terms on which this man-and-man relationship is to exist. It has also been called, "true manhood" and "empathic understanding." The Superior Man is the ideal each of us strives to attain. He is the pinnacle, the model that others will want to emulate.

"He is the only man who is real," said Confucius. He is the man of ethics and of shining quality.

Therefore, this man-and-man relationship (Jen) must exist on the terms of Chu-tse or the Superior Man. In short, what this means is that man-and-man relationships are founded on etiquette toward one another making it possible to harmonize society with friendship and love.

The third concept is called "Li." It has two distinct meanings.

The first is called propriety. Confucius realized that man, in his search for beauty and serenity and in his search for harmony (with Chu-tse), must start with something. To start from nothing is a much harder task, if not an impossible one, because good is so easily distracted by bad. So Confucius thought he might set down various precepts for the society. In this way each person might have something to use to guide him to be a better person. No person would ever be at a loss as to how to behave.

He did this by setting down numerous maxims. Through maxims and anecdotes, he tried to set down the way a person should pattern his life. He wanted people to have goals.

But before we use these maxims we have to know what rules and norms society has defined.

This is why the Doctrine of the Mean was so important. Mean translates as "middle" or "constant" (chung yung, in Chinese). Therefore, the Mean is the "way that is constantly in the middle," between life's extremes. This mean prevents excess and checks depravity before it occurs.

The second meaning of Li is ritual. When one responds properly to the Confucian maxims and the Mean, then his life becomes a stylized *ritual*, a ceremonial rite. The life is ordered and has meaning. This is not a dead, socially imposed kind of stylization, but a self-subjected betterment. Through this stylization there is peace with oneself and the universe that engulfs one.

The fourth concept is called "Te" or power.

Confucius disagreed with the Realists of his own time period that the only true government was through power. This then brings us to the question as to what is this enigma called power?

Confucius looked at power not as a means of physical weaponry but as metaphysical betterment and contentment. Power in this sense is within each of us to do what has to be done, and ability to carry out the concepts of Li.

This Te differs from the Te of the Taoists who believe it as a means of reason and virtue. The Confucian believes it as a means of self-understanding and a driving force to fling one into the realm of reality.

To the Confucians Te also meant virtue to some extent. Their virtue was the way a ruler should rule his people, a father his family, an elder a younger. The Taoist on the other hand regarded virtue in a mystical sense that held on to the understanding of the Tao. This understanding is a heavenly thing. The Taoist concern of heavenly virtue was looked down upon by the Confucians. Confucians believed that the world should be looked up to first and heaven will take care of itself.

The Taoist believed the opposite. They said that Heaven (Tao) is the main concern and the world can take care of itself.

Virtue to the Confucian also held standards of relationships. There are Five Relationships that are to be observed and held to be the first step in becoming a Superior Man. They are, in order of importance:

1. Father to son
2. Older brother to younger brother
3. Husband to wife
4. Elder to younger
5. Ruler to subjects

These Relationships must be so strong that they will pass beyond the barrier of death. Thus, a father even though dead must be respected. Also true is that an ancestor, even though dead for three hundred years, is still your elder and must be respected.

The last concept is called "Wen." This translates as the "arts of peace," as in opposition to the "arts of war."

Confucius was by no means an advocate of "art for art's sake." He cherished this axiom mainly as a means of moral education. He often said of music, "Music in the soul can be heard by all the universe."

CHAPTER THREE

"The Genius of the Absurd"

Next to the *Tao-Te-Ching* the most important writing in Taoism is the book ascribed to Chuang-tse. Very little is known of Chuang-tse and that little is inextricably woven into legend. It is said that he was a contemporary of Mencius. His personal name was Chou, and he was a native of Meng, where he once served in the petty position of "Official of the Lacquer Garden."[1] He lived in the same time as King Hui (370—319 B.C.) of Liang and King Hsuan (319—301 B.C.) of Ch'i. Chronologically this makes him a contemporary of Mencius.

Chuang-tse was to Lao-tse as Saint Paul was to Jesus and Plato to Socrates. He advocated "relativity" as the basis of all moral standards and ethical values.

The rhythm of life and its organic vision, an idea poetically put forth in the *Tao-Te-Ching*, is brought to perfect expression by the writings of Chuang-tse.

Most other philosophers were concerned with the laying down of practical conduct for the social norms and the ideals for running a good government. This can be seen in the writings of Confucius (principle of Li), and many other social philosophers of ancient China.

Chuang-tse transcended the illusory dust of the world (whang cheng, in Chinese), thus laying down the metaphysical foundations for a state of emptiness or ego transcendence. With great imagination and superb weaving of fantasy, he captured the depth, glory and color of Chinese thinking.

The essays and stories which constitute the *Book of Chuang-tse* go deeper into mysticism than those found in the *Tao-Te-Ching* anthology. We can find that in the doctrine there are continuous transformations within the body of the Tao (interpreted as the principle that embraces all of nature) and that these can be accounted for in terms of the two principles which had over the years been the foundation of Chinese thought and cosmology—the yin and yang.

YIN AND YANG

In the general sense the yin/yang philosophy is a theory of opposition. In the original meaning it meant "sunless" and "sunny." For example, the southern side of the mountain is yang and the northern side is yin; while the southern side of the river is yin and the northern is yang. In time they came to mean "female" and "male." Finally, they became general terms for the fundamental and opposing forces or principles of nature.

In the *I-Ching*, the yin and yang took on special significance. The yang came to represent the solid, continuous line, while the yin represented the broken line.

Therefore, the yang is all that is good: male, strong, light, inner-self etcetera, while the yin is bad: female, weak, dark, outer-self etcetera.

This is not to say that the ancient Chinese looked at the female as a dark, evil entity. They believed that all life was made up of two opposing forces interacting between themselves, giving the universe a substantive reality. Within the person there is both good and bad, there is conscious and unconscious. The fact that for the creation of a human being you need both a female and a male, leads to the idea of these two beings being opposing forces. Thus, there is no implication that the female is evil, only the categorization of her as being something biologically different from the man.

The symbol of the yin/yang is a circle with a twisted "S" in the middle. The wave in the "S" is to represent the principle of continuous movement/finite movement, of rising/lowering. Within the symbol of the yin/yang is a representation of its philosophy.

In the center of the dark area (representing "light," therefore yang) is a spot that appears as an eye. This shows there is a grain of yin in yang. The same holds true on the light side (representing dark, therefore yin); there is an element of yang, showing its presence. It is through the interaction of yin and yang that the universe and reality were created.

To show this interaction of yin in yang and yang with yin, we can turn to the second verse in the *Tao-Te-Ching* by Lao-tse:

> When beauty is known as beauty, lo
>   ugliness is there.
> When good is known as good, bad and good
>   together go.
> Thus something and nothing produce each other;
> The difficult and the easy complement each other;
> The short and the long offset each other;
> The high and the low incline towards each other;
> Note and sound harmonize with each other.
> Therefore, the sage in his affairs
>   does not on dwelling do,
> But proceeds in silence like the myriad of things
>   which come to be.
> Which growing, claim no ownership,
>   producing no rewards.
> And claiming not, assuming not,
>   continue ceaselessly.[2]

The polarity in the yin/yang can explain in a rough way the opposition between Confucianism and Taoism. The Confucians were activists and pursued the good in a positive way, as they thought best. The Taoists were passive, yin-like. They pursued good in a negative, passive way by the ideal of harmony with the Tao which would go beyond "good and evil." Let things be—such was their motto.

There are two major differences between the Taoism of Lao-tse and that of Chuang-tse.

The first was that judgments concerning right and wrong are, according to Lao-tse, said always to be made from different points of view, so that not only are different judgments concerning the same things made from different points of view but also it is impossible to decide on the relative merits of these different standpoints. As a solution, Chuang-tse suggests a higher point of view. These are treated as equally valid or, if you like, equally invalid. It follows that life is desirable and death is undesirable only from the point of view of the living. How then does one know that the reverse is not the case from the point of view of death? The result is the position that there is no reason to prefer one view to another.

Secondly, Chuang-tse shows great interest in the problem of whether there is something which is in effective control over mental activities such as sense perception. This mind or soul which is the elusive sovereign of the body seems to be thought of as a counterpart to the Tao which is the equally elusive sovereign of the universe.

OTHER CHINESE PHILOSOPHERS

MO-TSE

The Utilitarian school of Mo-tse was a strong, popular school in ancient times. Mo-tse disagreed with Confucius that goodness was the key to successful social organization, on the grounds that it was not sufficiently practical.

Mo-tse was also against the Confucian institutions, especially the Five Relationships (see concept of *Te* in Confucianism), charging that they were not sufficiently useful for achieving the well-being and happiness of the people. He felt that all institutions of society should be justified by their usefulness in promoting the welfare of men; at the same time, he believed that Heaven was deeply concerned with this welfare. He attempted to penetrate beyond the Five Relationships which Confucius thought were essential to the fabric of society and said what lies beyond all these is *love.*

He thought that war, hate and fear can all be conquered if men would act in a loving way towards each other. Each man should feel himself as one with each other man. This way, the sorrows and pains that are felt by one, should be felt by all. This way, man can grow with a respect and empathy towards all other men and thus achieve universal peace.

Mo-tse believed that his universal love corresponded to the will of God, and he proved this by saying that heaven loves righteousness and hates wickedness.

Mo-tse rejected ritual and luxury. The rejection of luxury carried into mistrust for the arts. He had little use for music, whereas Confucius thought that it was essential to emotion and social improvement.

HAN FEI TZU

The Legalist school, which is best represented by Han Fei Tzu, a student of Hsun-tse, advocated the establishment of infallible laws designed to meet the needs of the time. In his thought Han Fei combined the teachings of numerous schools to form the system known as the Legalist school of thought. It combined a "method of dealing with the subjects" advocated by Shen Pu-hai (king of Ch'in), "the rule of law," and the "exploitation of the vantage position of the ruler."

The key principle of the Legalist school was that rewards and punishments could be used to regulate and make good the action of people. It is not necessary to wait until people become good to have good behavior; good behavior can be produced through a system of law to which are attached rewards and punishments as sanctions.

CHU HSI

The philosopher Chu Hsi (1130—1200 A.D.) elaborated a system that bore certain analogies to Platonism (the philosophy of Plato, the Greek Philosopher) and that attempted to give a rational meaning to the universe.

A central concept in his metaphysics was that of li (not the li of Confucius, who meant it as "ceremony"). According to Chu Hsi, each entity has its li—the form that makes it what it is. The li of the members of the same species are identical; thus every tiger participates in or is shaped by the same li (li is similar to Plato's doctrine of Forms). What makes the difference between individuals is their Ch'i or vital energy.[†] This difference is very similar to the Greek's form-matter distinctions. It is possible, according to Chu Hsi, to see beyond li-chi's value and discover the underlying principle of all life which we shall call the "Ultimate Reality." It is called Tai Chi in Chinese, or the Supreme Ultimate.

[†]Ch'i can also be described as an intrinsic life force that is stored three inches below the navel in a storehouse called by various names: Tan Tien, Hara, Stahara, Shikataden and Kara. There are two kinds of Ch'i, Wei Ch'i, the Ch'i of the universe (as in Chu Hsi's description), and the Jun Ch'i, the Ch'i that flows within the body in channels called Meridians. There are twelve points on the Meridians when, at certain times of day, more Ch'i passes than at others. This Jun Ch'i is the principle on which the art of Seitaito (acupuncture) is based.

LU HSIANG-SHAN

A great figure in Neo-Confucianism was that of Lu Hsiang-Shan (1139—1192 A.D.), who moved Neo-Confucianism into idealism.

He differed from Chu Hsi in wishing to simplify the picture of the universe even further. While Chu Hsi analyzed the universe into two great principles, the li and Ch'i, Lu wished to trace the universe to one great principle. He claimed that the earlier philosophers had no duality in the universe, but regarded the universe as one organic whole. Lu argued that the only principle that underlies the universe is li. But this belief itself was mental in nature, not physical. Thus he claimed, "The universe and my mind are one; my mind and the universe are one."

Lu's philosophy was later perfected by Wang Yang-ming (1473—1529 A.D.), so that this school is called the Lu-Wang system.

Part Two
Buddhist Philosophy

"I gaze and gaze each passing day
    On the geranium sweet,
And for the happy day I yearn
    My Amida to meet.

If from the Buddha Amida
    My heart in coloring gains,
It will be like the beauteous boughs
    In autumn's crimson stains.

If in the winter of our sins
    Amida's name we call,
Warm rays from him will chase away
    The cold and snowdrifts all."

                    —Honen
                        on Amida Buddhism

CHAPTER FOUR

"The Enlightened One"

Buddhism was founded in the Sixth Century by Siddhartha Gautama, called the Buddha (Enlightened One), 563—483 B.C. It was founded in India and took its greatest hold in China and Japan.

Buddha's father, King Suddhodhana, lived in the Royal Palace in Kapilavastu. He was wealthy, a good ruler and all his people praised him. But to fulfill his happiness, the King wished for a child. Alas, he could have none.

He offered much sacrifice to the Hindu gods and studied much scripture to show the gods his purity. Then, at the age of fifty, the King had a son by his wife, Queen Maya, and called the newborn child, Siddhartha.

At the news of the Prince's birth, many holy men from all over India came to present their praise. Among the many visitors were Seven Holy Men from the Himalayan Mountains. When the King questioned them they all replied:

"What a beautiful child. No other like him has ever been born before." They could not take their eyes off the little Prince. Again and again they stared at the child, saying:

"He will grow up to be a very great man!"

"What do you see in my son's future?" questioned the King.

"If he chooses the worldly life, he will grow up to be great and rule the world."

The King was pleased and ordered more food to be served at the feast.

On the same day Prince Siddhartha was born, so one story tells, his future wife, the Princess Yosodhara, was also born.

And when the Prince was sixteen, old by standards of ancient India, he was to be wed. Being so learned and beautiful, the

Princess Yosodhara was chosen. This was an unusual coincidence.

On the request of his father, Siddhartha studied many Hindu scriptures: the *Vedas*, the *Brahmanas* and the *Upanishads*. The Prince was now quite content at studying the scriptures, living in the palace and having the most beautiful woman in all of India as his wife.

Yet there was in his unconscious a drive to learn more and a voice that kept telling him there was more to life than luxury.

One day while hunting with his bodyguard Channah, the Prince on his way home saw a man, all skin and bones, writhing in pain upon the ground.

"What is wrong with this poor man?" questioned the Prince to Channah.

"This man is sick and seems to be in great pain, my Prince!"

"But why is this man sick?"

"That, my Prince, is the way of all life. All become ill."

Siddhartha asked no more questions, but was very sad.

A few days later, when Siddhartha and Channah went out again, they met an old man, so old that his back was curved; his face and hands were as withered as a prune. He head nodded all the time. His hands shook as small trees in an earthquake.

"What is wrong with this man?" questioned the Prince.

"He is very old, my Prince."

"Is he sick and in pain?"

"No, my Prince, he is just old. This is the way of old age."

This time the Prince returned home, not only feeling sad, but sick.

The next day, when the Prince and Channah went out, they came across a funeral procession. The Prince seemed quite puzzled at this sight. Everyone was crying and feeling great sorrow.

The Prince asked Channah for an explanation.

"This, my Prince, is the way of every man. Be he leech, a king or a pauper, he will die. All die, my Prince, it is the way of life. Life is but a journey towards death."

When he went home his wife had planned a great feast in the palace. But the Prince was too tired and sick to eat. He retired to his study to meditate on what had been heard and seen the past three days.

All his life was spent in this palace, enjoying the good of life. He had been reared studying the great writings of the wise men, yet there was something missing.

Something must be wrong with life, he thought, to have old age, sickness, pain and death. In all the scriptures he had not seen nor read any explanation for these four things. He wondered why all the people in his kingdom could not be as kind, jolly and happy as he.

He learned that real life was not like it was in the palace; many people had it poor and hard. Siddhartha, for the first time in his life, began to realize how hard other people had it.

Siddhartha wondered why so many people were divided into so many classifications. This to him did not seem fair.

As he was thinking, he realized, as he heard the music from the hall, that pleasure was temporary, and all life ends in death. The more he meditated on this unhappiness and suffering in the world, the sicker he became.

The next day he went out again to the garden and met Channah. The two decided to go to the market place. Once there he saw many people begging for food and money. He recognized some of these beggars as priests who live in the mountains where their thoughts will not be disturbed. He wished that he could follow in their footsteps and have time to himself to meditate on the problem of suffering. It was then and there the Prince decided to leave the palace, his wife and son, and his wealth, and go out to the mountains to live like the poor monks.

It was the day his search for wisdom began.

THE ENLIGHTENMENT

At first the Prince—turned beggar—learned from the Brahmins (first in the caste system, the priests), and with five companions endured a long period of vigorous mortification of the flesh. He practiced asceticism, often fasting until he fainted. He grew weaker and weaker, but not one bit wiser. Finally he realized that this fasting did not produce wisdom and he began eating, allowing his strength to return. His mind became clearer and he continued his search.

One day he sat under a wild fig tree (called the Bo or Bodhi tree) to meditate, and allowed the views of his previous lives to pass before him. It was then he realized that the cause of all suffering in the world and the endless series of births and rebirths through which we pass, was self-craving and desire. Extinguish this and we are free from the Wheel of Life, birth, growth, decay and death. We would be free from endless suffering.

At this point, he wondered if others could be taught the wisdom he had just gained. Meditating, he decided to teach his five fellow students the wisdom that had lighted his path and destiny.

It wasn't long before his wisdom caught on and many came to hear him speak.

He told his followers that the first law is: from good must come good and from evil must come evil. To Siddhartha, this was the Key to Wisdom.

He realized this concept was not a new one, for it was the law of Karma,[†] taught by Hinduism. But from the old law he drew new conclusions. For seven days he remained under the Bo tree (translates as the Tree of Wisdom), preparing further knowledge.

At his first great sermon, called the Sermon of Benares, a monk asked him:

"Are you god?"

"NO!" answered Siddhartha.

"Then are you a saint?"

"NO!"

"If you are not a god and not a saint, what are you?"

"I am awake," Siddhartha told him.

Since that day the people who followed Siddhartha called him Buddha, which means "The Awakened One" or "The Enlightened One."

As his fame grew so did his followers. His disciples gathered and were sent forth to preach the word, the Dharma, to all mankind.

From these disciples the Buddha founded one organization which Buddhism knows—the Order of the Sangha. There are no priests, no creeds. This idea of priesthood and supernatural power is looked down upon by Buddhists.

All that a teacher can do is set an example for the student to follow. In this sense the teacher is not a priest but a philosopher showing the way to reality.

The Buddha gave his disciples a simple formula to teach their students.

[†] A law that from good you will receive good, from bad, bad in return. Karma decides what kind of life a person will be forced to lead in the afterlife. If you are good in this life, good is granted to you in the next and vice versa. In other words, you reap the rewards of your actions and efforts, be they good or bad. You cannot say that nothing or no one notices your actions, be they good or bad, because the force of Karma sees and hears all. Sometimes a person will wonder why an evil man in this world is receiving goodness and fortune, instead of misfortune as he deserves. Simple; he is still living out the goodness he had in the life before this one, but don't worry, he'll pay for it next time around.

I take refuge in the Buddha.
I take refuge in the Dharma (Teachings),
I take refuge in the Sangha (Order).

To illustrate this philosophy, let us look at a sermon the Buddha gave to the fire-worshipers of Uruvela. He used the subject of a recent jungle fire on a nearby hillside:

"All things are on fire; the eye is on fire, and whatever sensation originates in the impressions received by the eye is likewise on fire. And with what are these things on fire? With the fire of lust, anger and illusion (maya), with these they are on fire. And so with the mind. Wherefore the wise man conceives disgust for the things of the senses, and being divested of desire he removes from his heart the cause of suffering."[3]

This is in all reality the essence, the heart and the soul of Buddhist Philosophy.

When the Buddha died there was no successor appointed for five hundred years. The teachings of Buddhist Philosophy, handed down orally, comprised an elite tradition known as the secret doctrine of the Order (Sangha), or the Jewel within the Lotus. This doctrine has come to be called the "Middle Way."

This is the way that rejects both asceticism and worldliness. It lies between these opposites, a point of tension where there is complete peace. This way is not religion, nor is it the worship of gods. It is Philosophy.

Once when a young man came to Siddhartha and asked him endless religious questions, the Buddha asked him whether, if struck by an arrow, he would refuse to remove it before he found out who shot it.

The Way is not religious discussion. For as the Buddha said, "Those who say, do not know; while those who know, do not say."

The Way then is that of thought, mental discipline; it mixes metaphysics with philosophy and psychology. The Doctrine is a medicine to cure an illness, the sickness of illusions of reality.

BUDDHIST PHILOSOPHICAL TRUTHS

The Buddha prescribed some medicine to cure a disciple of his sufferings. The first step in the detachment from illusion is to understand the meaning of the soul. The soul has three states or Three Signs of Being.

Each of the Three Signs answers the question, What is the Soul? They are:

1. It is always becoming something new and losing what it is now,

2. It is always suffering, though it often conceals its suffering from itself, and

3. There is no enduring, permanent personality—spirit is not anyone's possession. It is the common denominator, that in which we all share, and this alone is permanent and eternal.

We crave life, and this attachment to worldly things, hoping to quench our craving thirst, is the force which drives us through endless rebirths. Birth leads to growth and growth to decay and decay to death and all the suffering that life entails. Then it all begins again, anew.

To stop this cycle of reincarnation (karma) we must quench desire; we must destroy the ignorance-produced, desire-maintained illusion of self which blinds us from life. In short, to escape this cycle of birth/rebirth we must follow the Four Noble Truths. This way, we may attain Nirvana, or the ceasing of reincarnation. In this sense the soul finds bliss and harmony with the universe. There is no duality between self/universe. The two know each other as one.

The Four Noble Truths:

The first is suffering. That is, old age is suffering; illness is suffering; death is suffering; being exposed to what one dislikes is suffering; being separated from what one likes is suffering; failure to realize one's ambitions and desires is suffering.

The second is desire. Suffering comes from the desire for being which leads to birth and rebirth, together with lust and desire, which find gratification here and there. The desire for being, the desire for pleasure and the desire for power—these are the sources of suffering.

The third is renunciation. Suffering can be dissolved with the complete annihilation of desire, separating and completely expelling one's self from it.

The fourth is the way, the truth and the life. The cessation of all desire can be gained by following the Eightfold Path.

The Eightfold Path:

Right Belief: Truth is the guide of the universe
Right Thought: keeping one's mind in the right perspective

Right Speech: cannot lie or slander anyone, never use coarse language

Right Conduct: never steal, kill or do anything you may later regret

Right Occupation: never choose an occupation that is considered against the philosophical Truths

Right Effort: always strive for what is good and not what is evil

Right Mind Control: of the Noble Truths, in calmness and worldly detachment

Right Meditation: will then follow and lead one on the right path of enlightenment.

Along with the Four Noble Truths and the Eightfold Path there is a set of ideas called the "Ten Commandments of Buddhism." These differ from the usual commandments of other philosophies and religions. They are a means of forcing the person away from the material desires of the world and attuning his mind towards ultimate reality. They are:

Do not destroy life.
Do not take what is not given to you.
Do not commit adultery.
Tell no lies and deceive no one.
Do not become intoxicated.
Eat temperately and not at all in the afternoon.
Do not watch dancing, nor listen to singing or plays.
Wear no garlands, perfumes or any adornments.
Sleep not in luxurious beds.
Accept no gold or silver.

Since these Ten Commandments were to lay down the pattern a life should form, I think a closer examination is merited.

Life to the Buddhist Philosopher is sacred. By life I mean not only the intellectual life of humans, but also the busy work-life of ants, bees and other insects. Each entity in the universe has a soul, a life substance. Since only the Universal Spirit can give this life substance, no human life can take it away. Each animal of nature has an order and a purpose. Since it has a purpose, it can be termed *necessary*. Therefore, all life is necessary and should not be destroyed.

Since a gift is a sign of faith to a person or an act of friendship, the gift in this sense is a friend only to the person who originally received it. It would be an act of unfriendliness to the whole of mankind if something is taken that is not yours.

Adultery is both harmful against yourself, the partner and the universe. To keep all in tune, adultery should be avoided.

Lies are the tools of misfortune. A lie will beget a lie and thus be a downfall of the original liar. Truth is a reflection of a man's soul. To lie is to blemish the cause of manhood and destroy the moral of one's self.

Intoxication is the act of a fool. To experience bliss when intoxicated is to escape from the world of reality. Intoxication is the tool of a man who is not one with himself, thus out of touch with the good of existence. There is no good in drinking for the feelings are false, illusions of the senses. Real bliss comes with Nirvana; there is no other.

Since there is a lack of food in this world, one should eat temperately. It is also true that the soul, when overfed, becomes lazy and does not try to achieve its full potential. A temperately fed soul is a fit soul, able to accomplish much. This way, fasting is a necessary endeavor to cleanse the body of waste, make the soul fit and tune the body with the mind. The afternoons should be set aside for the discovery of the truths, not for eating.

The body must not be disturbed by anything that will upset the harmony you are trying to achieve. Dancing and singing will upset this harmony since they are unnatural to the body. Music in turn is beneficial when played properly.

Garlands, perfumes and adornments are unnatural to the self and clutter one's natural beauty. Therefore, they should be avoided.

Sleep to strengthen the spirit and refresh the body. There is, therefore, no need for luxury.

Since the life of a Buddhist Philosopher is a poor, humble one, there is no need for gold or silver.

Infallible guides on the path of perfect peace are the Ten Perfections.

The first Perfection is Giving.

"As a jar overturned pours out the liquid and keeps back nothing, even so shall your charity be without reserve—as a jar overturned."

The second Perfection is Renunciation.

"As a cow, when the hair of her tail becomes entangled in

anything, would rather suffer death than injure her tail, even so you should keep to your principles as a cow to her tail."

The third Perfection is Duty.

"As a man in prison, suffering pain for long, knows that there is no pleasure for him but only to wait for release, so shall you look upon your existence on earth as prison, and turn your face towards your duty."

The fourth Perfection is Insight.

"As a beggar-monk shuns no families from whom he begs, whether lowly or high or in-between, and acquires his daily fare, so shall you at all times question the wise and gain insight."

The fifth Perfection is Courage.

"As the lion, king of the beasts, whether when lying down or standing up, lacks no courage, but is ever light-hearted, so shall you always hold true to your courage."

The sixth Perfection is Patience.

"As the earth bears all that is cast upon it, both the pure and the impure, and feels no resentment nor rejoicing, so also shall you receive favors and rebuffs alike with indifference."

The seventh Perfection is Truth.

"As a star of healing is balanced in the heavens and swerves not from its path in its time and its season, so also shall you remain fixed on your path of truth."

The eighth Perfection is Resolution.

"As the stone mountain, firmly based, quails not before the tempest but abides in its place, so also shall you abide in your resolution once resolved."

The ninth Perfection is Loving Kindness.

"As water quenches the thirst of the good and the bad alike and cleanses them of dust and impurity, so also shall you treat your friends and foes alike, with loving kindness."

The tenth Perfection is Serenity.

"As indeed the earth looks with serenity on all the purity and impurity cast upon it, even so shall you approach with serenity both joy and sorrow—as if you are to attain wisdom."

It is the goal of all Buddhist Philosophers to reach a state called Nirvana.

The word Nirvana means literally a blowing-out, as in the extinguishing of a candleflame. It is thus a negative form following upon the fulfillment of the Four Noble Truths. However, both the path and its goal (Nirvana) are referred to as more joy-giving than the life of perpetual creation of new sorrows by the operation of personal desire. The Buddha said of Nirvana:

"Enter the path! There is no grief like hate,
   No pain like passion, no deceit like the senses!
Enter the path! Far hath he gone whose foot
   Treads down one fond offense.
Enter the path! There spring the healing streams
   Quenching all thirst! There bloom the immortal flowers
Carpeting all thirst! There bloom the ways of joy. There
   Throng swiftest and sweetest hours!"

And there is also the personal testimony of Buddha:

"I, Buddha, who wept with all my brothers' tears,
Whose heart was broken by a whole world's woe,
   Laugh and am glad, for there is
   Liberty!
Ho! Ye who suffer! Know, ye suffer from yourself.
   None else compels . . . ."[4]

It is clear from this quotation that although Buddha would not approve of any positive description of Nirvana, he did so because it has no qualities conceivable by the mind, no comparison with anything thinkable or presented in the form of matter, and he has declared a positive and joyous knowledge. Indeed, the title "Buddha" arose from that, as it derives from the verbal root *budn*, to know. There is nothing negative about it, except that it cannot be perceived through the senses.

To try to put it into some form of words or wording, we would have to say that Nirvana is when the mind/spirit/body become one and this personal oneness then becomes one with the universe. There is happiness, good and contentment in this realization. When there is this realization, there is no need for rebirths (whose purpose is soul maturity), for the person is matured and thus is one and the same as his ULTIMATE REALITY.

Buddhism has passed through the most radical transformations since its inception. This should not disturb us. Philosophy and religion are not abstract truths handed down from the heavens. They are real, meaningful statements arising from human needs and therefore must be shaped and reshaped according to those needs. As society develops and conditions change, philosophy and religion, if they are to remain alive, must interpret those changes and modify themselves correspondingly. This has been the case with every philosophy, including Taoism, Platonism, Epicureanism—and Buddhism is no exception. It has been the case of every living religion, including Christianity—again Buddhism is no exception.

Since the Buddha left no successor and no ecclesiastical organization, there were a good number of various, different interpretations to his doctrines.

It was sixty years after the death of Gautama that his great teachings were committed to writing. These writings are called the *Sutras*, which consist of doctrines embodied in set phrases and parables.

The first great landmark in the early history of Buddhism is the work of Emperor Asoka (274–232 B.C.). He devoted his entire life to the spread of Buddhism as both a philosophy and a religion. He left his teachings of the Buddha on a number of stone tablets. These are considered the oldest surviving records of Buddhism and its doctrines.

The tablets include sermons and instructions on conduct: truth, obedience and respect for parents and living creatures. Asoka spread his writings from Kashmir to the Himalayas, from the borderlands on the Indus to Burma and Ceylon. The conversion of Ceylon established Buddhism in the center which became and remains the home of the most orthodox variety of the faith. In time, Buddhism disappeared from India proper.

By the beginning of the Christian Era, Buddhism was divided into two sects, the narrow and more orthodox Hinayana or Theravada of the South, and the broader Mahayana of the North.

Hinayana in literal translation means "Lesser Vehicle," while Mahayana means "Greater Vehicle." Hinayana is characteristically strict and exclusive, while the goal of Mahayana encompasses the satisfaction of the spiritual needs of all men.

The classical document of the Mahayana sect is the *Lotus Sutra*. It preaches the doctrine of the "Cosmic Buddha" in whom all things consist, who is frequently incarnated into saintly men called

Bodhisattvas. The ideal of Buddhahood is held out to all men and not merely to an elite few.

The Bodhisattvas are those followers of Buddha who have reached the point of illumination (self-realization/Nirvana) and have decided not to retire into bliss, but to continue in incarnation to help other living beings until all men are free.

HINAYANA AND MAHAYANA BUDDHISM

The practice of Hinayana Buddhism (whose members are often seen clad in yellow robes) is rational and ascetic; it holds no promise of future bliss and is devoid of all beauty—instead, cold, passionless and nonspeculative. Its scholars dislike arguing and often answer questions in the form of parables.

The Hinayana, like any sect, changed the original doctrines to suit their own personal needs. Indian Philosophy calls the Self of the universe Brahman, and yet it is at the same time the human soul or the Atman. Thus the psychic and the cosmic principles are one. The Hinayanaists say that the Atman cannot be described in words; it is incomprehensible and ought never to be mentioned. Hence Hinayana subscribes to the Anatta Doctrine which asserts the negation of the Atman, which may even mean the denial of the Atman conceived as a personal, immortal soul; perhaps even the denial of the absolute yet personal God. They believe it is better to deny its existence than corrupt that existence by trying to describe it. Hence, God and Soul are maintained in noble silence.

Hinayana Buddhism has found the greatest followings in Ceylon, Burma, Thailand and Indonesia. The term Hinayana is disliked by the monks because it implies that they are lesser than and inferior to the Greater Vehicle, or the Mahayana. They prefer the term Theravada, which means "Doctrines of the Elders."

The more liberal type of Buddhism called Mahayana has branched into many different forms, each adapted to the needs of large groups of worshipers. It is both positive, as contrasted with the negative attitudes of the Anatta Doctrine, and speculative.

It manages to combine a particularly exalted form of mysticism with an almost sensual appeal to the multitude.

The major doctrine and belief of the Mahayanaists is the belief that salvation can be found within the Wheel of Becoming, whereas for orthodox Buddhism salvation is precisely the same as escape from Samsara, the endless series of births and rebirths in the world of temporal and material life. For the Mahayanaist, Nirvana is not the goal of escapism, a refuge from the Turning Wheel (Samsara); it *is* the Wheel, and he who realizes himself in this discovery makes his daily life divine.

Mahayana also has a mystical or paradoxical side that is referred to as Esoteric Buddhism or Esoteric Mahayana. It says that all things can be reduced to pairs of negatives. That is: no birth, no death; no oneness, no manyness; no coming into being, no going out of existence. If this seems nonsense to the senses, then reason is useless and we must turn to intuition. To understand, the mind must learn to hold the opposites in living motion and continual union. If you analyze a flower petal by petal, there is no flower; hold a handful of sea, and the sea is no more.

It is very difficult to put the doctrines of Mahayana into words. It is because of this that many on the path fall and are broken on the climb. *But each man is the way*, and only "he who loseth his life shall find it." This, then, is mysticism, the life of philosophy. Without this mysticism, Mahayana Philosophy loses the reason for its existence, the mystical "neither-one-nor-many." "It is beyond the conception of human reason," one scholar said. Mysticism is essential to the philosophy of Mahayana, for without it there would remain nothing but the cold ashes of death.

The ideas, beliefs and the soul of Esoteric Mahayana Buddhism can be summarized philosophically as follows:

The Godhead is beyond all predicates. It is neither that which is existent, nor nonexistent, neither one nor many. It is beyond the conception of human reason.

The abstract principle and its manifestations are two parts of one whole, the Wheel of Becoming. Our limited, temporal, terrestrial existence does not stand in contrast to Nirvana. It is a mode of existence of Nirvana, which need not be sought by denying existence.

All manifestations of the absolute are illusory and ephemeral; all the appearances of phenomenal reality have no essential being and must not be regarded as what is.

Not even Nirvana can be said to exist, because nothing can be said about it. Even the Buddha and his Doctrines do not exist in this sense. They only appear to exist on a lower plane of understanding. This doctrine of emptiness (Sunyata) is the greatest principle in Mahayana Philosophy. (You will read more about it when we come to speak of Zen.)

Even the teachings of the Buddha are affected by this truth. He really had no doctrine, because what he expressed in terms of law is inexpressible, and is impossible, and therefore all that has been said cannot be said in any language.

The major differences between Hinayana and Mahayana (excluding Esoteric Mahayana) Buddhism can be summed up in the following:

1. Hinayana holds that man is on his own in this universe, there being no superhuman gods or powers to help him over the humps. For Mahayana, in contrast, grace is a fact. Peace can be at the heart of all because of a boundless power underlying all the principles and giving all life.

2. Hinayana considers man as basically an individual, his emancipations not contingent upon the salvation of others. Mayahana says the opposite: Life being all one, the fate of one individual is the fate of all others.

3. In Hinayana the key virtue is Bodhi, wisdom with the absence of self-seeking emphasized more than the active doing of good. Mahayana moved another word to the center: Karuna, or compassion. Unless compassion is at the center, wisdom is useless.

4. Theravada Buddhism centers around the monk. Monasteries are the spiritual foci for the transmission of the Bodhi. Mahayana, on the other hand, is a philosophy and a religion for the layman.

5. The ideal of the Hinayanaist is the Arhat, the perfected disciple who, wandering like the lone rhinoceros, strikes out towards the goal of Nirvana. The Mahayana ideal, on the contrary, is the Bodhisattva, "one whose essence is perfected wisdom."

6. The last major difference is the way the Buddha himself is looked at. To Hinayana Buddhism, the Buddha is a Saint; to the Mahayana Buddhist, the Buddha is a Savior.

We can schematize the differences which divide the two great branches of Buddhism as follows:

Theravada	Mahayana
Religion is the concern of monks.	Religion is the concern of everyone.
Buddha as a Saint and Teacher.	Buddha as a Savior.
Avoid ritual and prayer.	Complex ritual accompanied by personal prayer.
Man is on his own in the universe.	Man is not alone.

VIRTUE: Wisdom.	VIRTUE: Compassion.
Religion and philosophy are a full-time job.	Religion and philosophy are relevant to the life in the world.
IDEAL: The Arhat.	IDEAL: The Bodhisattva.
Eschews metaphysics.	Elaborates metaphysics.
Conservative.	Liberal.

TYPES OF THERAVADA SCHOOLS

1. THE SAUTRANTIKAS

The Sautrantikas belong to the Theravada branch of Buddhism. Their name comes from their claim that they follow only the ORIGINAL sutras of the Buddhist Scriptures, but not any of their commentaries (by later, so-called authorities). They are a division of a wider branch of Theravada called Sarvastivadins (their central doctrine is that everything exists). In other words, the school of Sarvastivadins is a branch of Theravada, and the Sautrantikas are a branch of the Sarvastivadins.

Some Sarvastivadins seem to have held the belief in "eternal atoms," but such a doctrine seems to conflict with the main doctrine of momentariness. Existence is found in being (satta) as opposed to the doctrine of mere flow (change, becoming, Samsara), and, therefore, even the doctrine that everything has existence (satta, astita) was not considered to be in accordance with the original Buddhist teachings.

The Sautrantikas maintain that, although everything exists and is real, it cannot be directly perceived, but only inferred. What can be directly perceived are sensations, ideas etcetera, but the real objects are behind them and their existence must be inferred. Their doctrine of perception is called the "Representative Theory." It states that the ideas we receive from objects, when we perceive them, are representations of them.

2. THE VAIBHASIKAS

The Vaibhasikas are also a branch of the Sarvastivadins. Their name comes from their claim of following the commentaries (vibhasas) to the *Tipitakas* (*Three Basket Doctrine*), whereas the Sautrantikas follow the Scriptures of the *Tipitakas*. They differ mainly by asserting that the objects are perceived directly, but not inferred. They uphold the doctrine of "Direct Perception," which states that all objects are perceived as they are, directly; there is no need for discrimination.

3. THE ANDHAKAS

The Andhakas were an interesting sect of Hinayana Buddhism and added greatly to the development of Mahayana. It is sometimes said that the *Prajnaparamitas* (see Glossary), the basic scripture of the Mahayana School, was first written by the Andhakas.

They believed that:

a) Everything, including the physical body, is only the mind. It exists when we are "mindful" of it. If we do not think of it, it is not there.

b) Because they were able to meditate for long periods of time, they felt that consciousness, as a single state, lasts for a long time.

c) Nirvana is only an inborn instinct, because it is eternally present within us; and the desire to attain Nirvana is an inward pull present in every human being, although appearing at times as only the desire for calm and quietness.

Through these ideas, the Andhakas paved the way for Buddhist idealism and absolutism. If Nirvana can be attained through meditation, then it must be conscious. It is, thus, consciousness.

TYPES OF MAHAYANA SCHOOLS

1. THE VIJNANAVADINS

They are also called the Yogacaras, because they believe in the importance of Yogic meditation. Ch'an and Zen Buddhism of China and Japan are a direct offshoot of the Vijnanavada school.

The founder of the Vijnanavada school is said to be Maitreyanatha, of the First Century A.D. Great exponents of the school, and great contributors, were Asanga and Vasubandhu, of the Fourth Century A.D.

The Vijnanavadins contend that, since Nirvana is the highest bliss without suffering, it must be a conscious state, because without consciousness happiness cannot be experienced. This state of consciousness (vijnana) is without any determination and it is its indeterminateness that is called emptiness (Sunyata). Although this consciousness (vijnana) is something to be attained by man, it is the source of everything determinate. Everything determinate is only a transformation of its original consciousness. This consciousness is, therefore, the Absolute.

Now if the Absolute Consciousness is the only reality, what makes it undergo transformations and become the plurality of objects? The Vijnanavadins say that transformation is not real; it is only Maya, or an illusion. We think that this world is real; but it is only a creation of Maya or Avidya, the principle of the Unconscious in us, which creates both our finite being and the objects around us.

The Vijnanavadins developed an epistemology (the study or the theory of nature and the grounds for knowledge with reference to its limits and its validity) that accorded with their metaphysics.

They believed that perception and inference were valid sources of knowledge, but added that the ultimate truth (Absolute Consciousness) can be directly known only by intuition, because mere reason, which is used in inference, always ends up in self-contradictions and cannot make a decision as to the existence of absolute truth.

2. THE MADHYAMIKAS

Like the Vijnanavadins, the Madhyamikas form one of the two most important schools of early Mahayana Buddhism. This school was founded by Nagarjuna, a monk who lived in the Second Century A.D. Nagarjuna's work, the *Madhyamikakarikas*, is the most important work in Buddhist Philosophy. It became the source of inspiration to the dialecticians in India. It was the first work in the history of world philosophy that tried to show the self-contradictory nature of every concept and doctrine about reality.

The aim of Nagarjuna was to show that nothing positive or negative can be asserted about reality; it is therefore emptiness (Sunyata). Even to think of it as Sunyata is a mistake, because the concepts of vacuity and emptiness are understood in Eastern philosophy as meaning fullness. Then there are two opposing forces, emptiness and fullness. But Sunyata is beyond all opposites; otherwise, it cannot be Nirvana and the goal of existence; and so reality should not be called by the name Sunyata also. Yet we call it Sunyata because we have to denote it, not connote it, by some word.

Nagarjuna took up all the concepts and doctrines of rival schools and exposed their self-contradictory nature. He spared none, not even the Buddha himself, and showed that all are self-contradictory and false. Nothing determined can be true and can express the nature of reality. Reality is unique and even the concept of uniqueness is not applicable to it.

Nagarjuna does not like to call Sunyata by its name Vijnana, because to call Sunyata consciousness is to characterize it, but Sunyata is without characterization.

Nagarjuna repeated continually that Sunyata is not nothingness, because he rejected both alternatives. He called himself a Madhyamika or a middlepather. Sunyata is not without value; it is the source of infinite possibilities because it is neither negative nor positive. Sunyata also means zero, and its neutrality (not negative or positive) can be seen in the zero. . . . -5, -4, -3, -2, -1, 0, 1, 2, 3, 4, 5, . . . The zero stands between -1 and 1, and thus it is neither.

OTHER FORMS OF BUDDHISM

AMIDA BUDDHISM

The Pure Land Sect, sometimes called Amida Buddhism, after its Japanese name, was reputedly founded in China by Hui-yuan in the latter part of the Fourth Century A.D., but its roots go back to devotional Buddhism expressed in the Indian scriptures, the *Sukhavati-vyusha Sutras*, which the school took as its authorization and uses as its major text. Its doctrine depends on the notion that merit can be transferred; especially can a great Buddha transfer merit to an otherwise unworthy devotee. Salvation, then, does not depend upon one's own power, but on the power of another.

The mythology of this sect centers around the Buddha of the Boundless Light, Amitabha. He was the focus of popular devotion and sentiment, though sometimes his place was overshadowed by the gentle figure of Kuan-yin. The cult of Amitabha expressed a very simple reliance on the grace of the Divine Power, for it is enough to utter his name with faith to be assured of paradise.

In Japan this sect is called Jodo Buddhism and was founded by Honen (1133—1212 A.D.). The principles of Jodo and Amida Buddhism are basically the same and thus to define one is to define the other.

Both allow for salvation through another, not by one's own merits. Particularly, there is the practice of nembutsu, which is daily repetition of "Namo Amitabha" ("Namu-Amida-Butsu," in Japanese Jodo). This is accompanied by a belief in salvation for all through trust in Amida (Buddha), because the Buddha-nature is present in all, and because in fact all and each are indissolubly together always.

One need only say the word, "Amida," and one is saved. This is because the Buddha-nature is in everyone, so by saying "Amida" you are invoking your True Self.

The reward is the Western Paradise or the Pure Land, which is the goal of anyone on the path of Amida Buddhism. This is achieved by devotion (bhakti) to the Buddha, rather than by work (karma) for the world. It is a more materialistic Heaven than a state of bliss as in Nirvana. Amida is in all reality a Bodhisattva, and it is believed that the accumulated merits of Amida and other Pure Land Saints can be transferred to the believer by simply reciting his name.

SHINGON BUDDHISM

Shingon Buddhism is a Japanese Buddhist sect which is highly mystical and syncretistical in nature. It was founded in 806 A.D. by Kobo Daishi. The deities and demons of other religions are interpreted as manifestations of the Dainichi Buddha, whose body comprises the whole of the universe. Cosmic mysteries are represented and visibly symbolized in tangible forms. The postures and the movements and the utterances of an elaborate ritual evoke these mysterious powers to its followers. The mysteries of the cosmos are graphed and symbolized in diagrams called Mandala, which symbolize two aspects of the universe: (1) its ideal or potential entity and (2) its vitality or dynamic manifestation.

KEGON BUDDHISM

Hua-yen, in Chinese. This school was introduced into Japan by the Korean monk Jinjo (died, 742 A.D.) and played a very important role during the Nara Period. Based on the *Avatamsaka Sutra*, Kegon Buddhism preaches the doctrine of Buddhahood of all sentient beings, Nirvana and Samsara, and wisdom and compassion of the Bodhisattvas who guide errant beings to Buddhahood. This school has had a considerable influence on the principles of Zen Buddhism. Its teachings say that the aim of Buddhism is to dispel illusion (Maya) of the separate ego (called Cosmotheism).

This school has ten basic principles, which are called the Ten Mysterious Gates, used in the exposition of its philosophy of totality.

These Ten Gates are described in the *Avatamsaka Sutra*: "The Buddha said, 'There are ten things by which beings do good and and ten things which they do bad. What are they? Three are performed by the mouth, four by the body and three with the mind. The (evils) performed by the body are killing, stealing and unchaste deeds; those with the mind are covetousness, anger and foolishness; those with the mouth are duplicity, slandering, lying and idle talk.' These ten things are not in keeping with the holy way and are called the Ten Evil Practices. Putting a stop to these is called the Ten Virtuous Gates."

To understand Kegon we must get well acquainted with the two key terms Ji and Ri. Ji (shih, in Chinese) means ordinarily "an event," a "happening," but in Buddhist Philosophy, the "individual," the "particular," the "concrete," the "monad;" while Ri (li, in Chinese) means "a principle," "reason," "the whole," "the all," "totality," "the universal," "the abstract" etcetera. Ji always stands contrasted to Ri and Ri to Ji. In regular Buddhist terminology, Ri corresponds to Sunyata, Void or Emptiness (kung, in Chinese; ku, in Japanese). The distinction made in Greek Philosophy between matter and form may also apply to that between Sunyata and Rupam. Ji is Rupam, form (se in Chinese; shiki, in Japanese), thus Sunyata, the void, contrasts to Rupam, the form. In other words, Ri to Ji.

According to Buddhist Philosophy, Ri or Ku (Sunyata) is characteristic first of emptiness or void. Emptiness does not mean absence in the same sense that there was something before and nothing now. Emptiness is not a somewhat existing besides something, it is not a separate independent existence, nor does it mean extinction. It is always with individual objects (ji); it coexists with form (rupam). Where there is no form there is no emptiness (Sunyata). For emptiness is formlessness and has no selfhood, no individuality, and therefore it is always with form. Form is emptiness and emptiness is form. If emptiness were something limited, something resisting, something impure in the sense of allowing something else to get mixed with it, it would never be with form, in form, and form itself. It is like a mirror; as it is empty and is holding nothing of its own, it reflects anything in it that appears before it. Emptiness is again like a crystal, thoroughly pure and transparent; it has no particular color belonging to it; therefore it takes any color that comes before it.

The principle of emptiness is best explained with a tea cup.

Nan-in was sitting down one afternoon drinking tea. A stranger came up, sat down and said, "I have heard you are skilled in the field of Zen, is this not so?"

Nan-in bowed to him.

"Then I have come to learn Zen from you, old man."

Master Nan-in consented and tried for many months to teach the young lad. But the boy's past training in Tendai Buddhist Philosophy affected his studies. Every time Nan-in explained a principle of Zen the youth would say, "In Tendai we believe this," or "In Tendai this is so."

Nan-in was fed up and sat down one evening to have tea with his student. He poured his cup normally but overpoured his student's till it overflowed on the table and his robes.

He shouted, "STOP! My cup is full! It cannot hold any more tea."

Nan-in looked at his companion. "Unless you empty your cup first, how can you ever taste my tea?"

The Kegon Philosophers,† like all other Buddhists, do not believe in the reality of an individual existence, for there is nothing in our world of experience that keeps this identity for even a moment; it is subject to constant change. Therefore, through emptiness, they are one with all and are at peace with the universe. They are content and live each moment, no matter how insignificant to another, as if it were a major happening. For to the Kegon Philosopher, all is important.

TENDAI BUDDHISM

Tendai is a school of Japanese Buddhism (T'ien T'ai, in Chinese). It was introduced to Japan from China by Dengyo Daishi (born about 767 A.D.), in about 805. He emphasized universality of salvation or attainment of Buddhahood. He established a great Tendai center on Mt. Hiei, near Kyoto; for centuries it remained the greatest center of Buddhism in Japan. With Shingon, Tendai was the leading force of religious faith and philosophical thought in Japan. Its teachings are based on the *Lotus Sutra* (*Hokkekyo*, in Japanese).

The Tendai doctrine speaks of a Threefold Truth, the three being three-in-one. These are: (1) the truth that all things are of the Void, because they are dependents in the stream of causation

---

†Kegon translates as "flower decoration."

and thereby not things in themselves, (2) the truth that the phenomenal existences of all kinds are only temporal productions and so only the Void—not real or self-existent, (3) that as everything involves everything else, all is one, and something of everything is the basis of being, this something being the Buddha-nature.

Because of the doctrine, Tendai believes that there is salvation for all, but not by either production or destruction of the character or qualities of anything. Because this doctrine comes from the *Lotus Sutra* (*Saddharmapundarika*, in Sanskrit), the school is sometimes called the Lotus school. In China it is very popular and sometimes mixes with the Pure Land sect.

The Tendai school advocates the practice of the "Ten Hands." They are steps and observances in meditation. The goal of the Tendai meditation is to become at perfect peace and attain Buddhahood. They are:

1. External conditions should be still and out of reach.
2. Control all sense desires, i.e., think of nothing; allow all noise to pass beyond the ears; see nothing; forget your surroundings.
3. Abolish all inner hindrances.
4. Regulate and adjust your body and mind—the body to the meditative techniques, the mind to the Scripture you are meditating on.
5. Expel activities of the mind.
6. Always use right practice.
7. Develop good qualities.
8. Destroy all evil influences.
9. Cure your diseases.
10. Realization of Supreme Ultimate Enlightenment.

If these ten steps or stages are faithfully followed, the mind will become tranquil, difficulties will be overcome, powers for concentration, insight and understanding will be developed and in the future Supreme Ultimate Enlightenment will be attained.

NICHIREN BUDDHISM

Nichiren Buddhism was founded by Nichiren, an outstanding figure in the religious history of Japan. A prophet, a missionary and a reformer, he established this system of Buddhism, named after himself, in 1253. In his youth he studied many scriptures trying to find the ultimate truth of reality and the true doctrine of Buddhism. Disgusted by corruption in the Buddhist hierarchy, the divisions between the sects and the calamitous state of the country, Nichiren, at age thirty, was convinced that true Buddhism is enshrined in the *Lotus* scripture. He denounced all other sects of Buddhism, saying, "Jodo sect and Honen himself are hell and evil, Zen is the devil, Shingon will cause national collapse, and Kegon is the enemy of the country."

He called on the government to suppress false teachings and be converted to the doctrine of the *Lotus Sutra*. With fervent zeal he preached in temples and marketplaces. Persecuted, attacked by mobs and exiled, suffering cold and hunger, he was sustained by his sense of mission. He attracted a large following: the sect continues today.

He emphasized three basic teachings:

1. Utterance of the *Lotus* scripture has mantic (divinatory) power. Namu-Myoto-renge-kyo is the passage. Meditation on this formula has deteriorated so that simple repetition is deemed sufficient for attaining enlightenment.

2. The graphic and symbolic representation of the Supreme Being who is the Buddha in his metaphysical entity, inherent in every being, the oneness of the Buddha-nature and its inexhaustible manifestations.

3. Need to establish a Holy Center, a central sect of universal Buddhism, which is to rule the world throughout the ensuing ages.

Nichiren's Buddhism was supposed to unify all Buddhism, but it brought about the formation of several sects.

CHAPTER FIVE

"Zen Buddhism"

There is perhaps no other form of Buddhism that has affected the people, art and culture of the Orient quite like Zen. Its simplicity has caused it to be mixed with arts of beauty, like painting and poetry, and arts of war, like karate and ken-jutsu (fencing). Its impact on the world was devastating and its effects will be eternal.

A HISTORY

Zen Buddhism was founded by an Indian monk named Bodhidharma.[†] Bodhidharma is an obscure figure in the history of China and India. The most reliable sources for our knowledge of the man are generally considered to be:

> Biographies of the High Priests, by Priest Tao-hsuan, written in A.D. 654
>
> The Records of the Transmission of the Lamp, by Priest Tao-yuan, written in 1004.

These seemingly authentic sources notwithstanding, modern scholars have either been reluctant to accept any single version of Bodhidharma's existence, or they assert that all accounts of the Indian monk are legendary. Yet eminent Buddhist-historians like D.T. Suzuki feel that Bodhidharma was an actual person despite the many myths that have been added to his biography.

Bodhidharma was the third child of King Sugandha of Southern India, was a member of the Kshatriya, or Warrior Caste, and had his childhood in Conjeeveram (also, Kanchipuram or Kanchee-

[†]Also called: Ta mo, Dharuma, Daruma Taishi, and Lo-han.

puram), the small but dynamic Buddhist province south of Madras. He received his training in Buddhist meditation from the master, Prajnatara, who was responsible for changing the young disciple's name from Bodhitara to Bodhidharma.

Bodhidharma was an excellent pupil and soon surpassed his fellow students. By middle age he was already considered a Buddhist master. When Prajnatara died, Bodhidharma set sail for China. Two reasons are given for his leaving. The first was a deathbed wish from his old master. The second was his own decision to go to China because he was saddened by the decline of Buddhism in the areas outside of India proper.

Accounts of Bodhidharma's activities in China vary considerably with the references cited. Tao-hsuan's *Biographies of the High Priests* states that Bodhidharma first arrived in China during the Sung Dynasty (420—479) of the Southern Dynasties (420—589), and later traveled north to the Kingdom of Wei. But the traditional date of Bodhidharma's entry into China has been 520 (or 526, 527). This appears to be rather late if Tao-hsuan's *Biographies of the High Priests* is accurate in placing him at the Yung-ning Temple at Lo-yang in 520. *Biographies of the High Priests* further states that a Buddhist novice called Seng-fu joined Bodhidharma's following, was ordained by Bodhidharma and then left to travel to Southern China where he died at age sixty-one. Basic arithmetic tells us that if Seng-fu were, indeed, sixty-one in 524, and had been the minimum acceptable age for ordination (twenty years old), he would have been twenty in 483, putting the Indian monk in China earlier than the traditional date.[5]

A variation of the above theory, found in the *Records of the Transmission of the Lamp*, places Bodhidharma in Canton in 527. After some time there, he traveled north, meeting Emperor Wu of the Liang Dynasty (502—557) at Ching-ling (now Nanking).

When Wu saw Bodhidharma he asked him:

"I have brought the Buddhist Scriptures from your country to mine. I have built temples of great beauty, and have seen to it that all under me learn the principles. What rewards will I receive in the next life for this?"

Bodhidharma answered, "None!"

The King was so angered that he banished Bodhidharma from the palace. Bodhidharma again headed north.

He traveled to Honan Province and visited the Shaolin (Sil-lum) temple on Mt. Shao-shih in the Sung mountain range.

On arriving at the Shaolin temple, he meditated in front of a wall for nine years. In this meditation Bodhidharma was so in tune with the laws of nature that it is said he heard the conversation of ants.

When he awoke he laid down the foundations to a new system of Buddhism, later to be called Zen.

Bodhidharma himself was the first patriarch of Zen, but the 28th patriarch of Buddhism. The others before him were:

1. Sakyamuni (the Buddha)	15. Kanadeva
2. Mahakasyapa	16. Arya Pahulata
3. Ananda	17. Samghanandi
4. Sanavasa	18. Samghayasa
5. Upagupta	19. Kumarata
6. Dhritara	20. Jayata
7. Micchaka	21. Vasubandhu
8. Buddhanadhi	22. Manura
9. Buddhamitra	23. Haklenasyasa
10. Bhikshu Parvsa	24. Bhikshu Simha
11. Punyayasas	25. Vasasita
12. Asvaghosta	26. Punyamitra
13. Bhikshu Kapimala	27. Prajnatara
14. Nagarjuna	28. Bodhidharma

From this we can see the complete transmission of enlightenment from the original Buddha down to Bodhidharma himself. This table is called the patriarchal line.

The next great development in Zen (that is, after the initial founding) came with the birth of the sixth patriarch, Hui-neng (638—713 A.D.). He came from Hsin-chou in the southern part of China. When he was very young his father died. He went to work and never finished his formal education. One day while selling wood, he came to a house where he heard someone reciting a Buddhist Scripture. The words touched him deeply; his heart began to flutter. Finding what the sutra was, Hui-neng was determined to learn it. The sutra was the *Diamond Sutra* or the *Vajracchedika-sutra*, and the man who was reciting it was Hun-jeng, the fifth patriarch of Zen.

Hui-neng managed enough money to support his mother properly. He then decided to reside in the temple to study the *Diamond Sutra*. When he arrived at the Yellow Plum temple in

Chin-chou he went to see Hun-jeng to ask his permission. Hun-jeng told him:

"Where do you come from?"

"I am a farmer from Hsin-chou and I wish to become a Buddha."

"You are a southerner," said Hun-jeng. "Southerners have no Buddha-nature."

This did not discourage Hui-neng. He told the master, "There are southerners and northerners, but as far as Buddha-nature is concerned, how can you make such a distinction?"

This pleased the master and Hui-neng was given the job as rice-pounder for the brotherhood.

After Hui-neng had been at the Yellow Plum temple for eight months, Hun-jeng announced that he was looking for a spiritual successor. Shen-hsiu (died 706) was the most learned of the monks. Most thought he would gain the successorship. Shen-hsiu composed a poem to show the master his knowledge and hung it on the wall of the meditation hall. It read:

> "This body is a Bodhi-tree,
> The soul is like a mirror bright;
> Take heed to keep it always clean,
> And let no dust collect on it."

All those who read the lines were greatly impressed, and secretly cherished the thought that the author of the gatha (poem) would surely be the next patriarch. Hun-jeng himself thought this.

The next day when they awoke, in the meditation hall right next to Shen-hsiu's gatha was another. It read:

> "There is no Bodhi-tree,
> Nor a mirror bright;
> Since all is void,
> Where can the dust alight?"

The master upon seeing this knew the author had more insight into the field of Zen than even himself. The author turned out to be a lowly layman, a cook. His name, Hui-neng.

At this Hun-jeng decided to transfer his robe to Hui-neng and call him the sixth patriarch. He had, however, some great misgivings concerning the matter; for the majority of his students were not enlightened enough to see anything of deep philosophical value in the lines of the rice-pounder, Hui-neng; and if he were awarded the robe publicly, they might do him harm. So Hun-jeng told Hui-neng to come to his room at midnight and it was there the transfer took place. That night, Hui-neng left the temple.

Three days after the flight of Hui-neng from the Yellow Plum temple, the news of what had happened in secret was known throughout the temple, and a party of monks led by one named Ming, pursued the fugitive, Hui-neng, who, in accordance with Hun-jeng's instructions, was silently leaving the brotherhood. He was apprehended by the monks as he passed a bridge near the temple. Hui-neng laid the robe down across a rock and told Ming:

"This robe is a symbol of the patriarchal faith and it is not to be carried away by force. Take it with thee, however, if thou so desirest."

Ming tried to lift the robe off the rock, but it was immovable. Ming trembled with awe. At last he shouted to Hui-neng, "I come here to obtain faith and not the robe. Oh brother, spare my ignorance."

"If you have come in faith, stop your babbling. Think not of good, think not of evil, but see what at this moment is thine original face. The face thou hadst at thy birth."

At this, Ming understood the truth of things and of Zen. Ming left in faith.

The principle ideas that have made Hui-neng the real founder of Chinese Zen (called Ch'an) may be summed up as follows:

1. We can say that Zen has come to its own consciousness under Hui-neng. While Bodhidharma was the first to bring the principles of Zen from India to China, they were weak and underdeveloped; they were not able to present themselves to the Chinese mind. It took over two hundred years for these principles to become tangible to the Chinese mind and for a man like Hui-neng to make this all clear. Hui-neng's Zen was for the purpose of "seeing into your own nature," not the liberation from Samsara.

2. Hui-neng stressed *abrupt* awakening. This seeing is an instant act, not something gained with years at a monastery.

3. Seeing into your own nature is something that results from intuition, not stylized meditation, which to Hui-neng was just quietistic time-wasting. There is nothing to this meditation other than tranquilization of the mind; there is no philosophy.

4. Hui-neng's method of demonstrating the truth of Zen was purely Chinese and not Indian. There was no abstract terminology nor romantic mysticism. His method was direct, plain and to the point.

WHAT IS ZEN?

Zen in its essence is the art of seeing into the nature of one's own being, and it points the way from bondage to freedom. The aim of Zen therefore is enlightenment (satori): the immediate, unreflective grasp of all reality, without logic and intellectualization; the realization of the oneness of man and the universe. This is the pre-intellectual grasp of a child, but on a new level, that of the full development of man's logic, reason and senses, his individuality. While a child's experience is that of immediate oneness before the alienation into the norms of society, the enlightenment experience lies after that.

Zen comes from the Chinese word, "Ch'an," which is a short form of the word, "Ch'an-na." Ch'an-na is the corruption of the Sanskrit word Dhyana and the Pali word Jhana. From this we can see that the pronunciation of Zen comes from a series of mispronunciations.

* * *

"In the landscape of spring
    There is neither high nor low;
  The flowering branches grow naturally,
    Some long, some short."

The beauty expressed in the above poem is taken from the *Renin*, a famous Zen work. It expresses the absolute nothingness and similarity of the spring setting. There is peace in the above situation and an immense totality of both reality and motion.

Yet the simplicity of the senyoto (four-line Zen poem) and the ultimate reality of Zen are much different in many ways, yet in others they are so similar I need not define further.

Bodhidharma wrote:

"No fixed doctrines;
    Without words or letters;
  Direct link to the mind,
    and the ultimate transformation to Buddhahood."

Perhaps this poem sums up the meaning of Zen.

Zen can be defined as a philosophy that centers around the turning of one's mind back to its original position, the time in childhood where all could be grasped because there was no relation to the logical intellect. Every act was from emotion or intuition. The child does not ponder each and every phase of his life, but flows freely from one activity to another. There is no stopping at any one point; if there were, there would be hesitation and indecision, common ailments of maturity.

Instead, all is free in movement and in contact with the oneness of the Self.

Zen is without scriptures, for it is said there is no set method. Each person is an individual and in order for him to reach satori he needs a path that is suited to himself. One path is not the answer. A system that has no method but *all methods*, no doctrines, and has no reason but reason (self-realization) seems to be in contradiction.

According to Master Basso:

> "To know myself
> within myself.
> What did I say?"

Another master, Hakuin, said: "Zen is a ball afloat on a stream, unsinkable, but yet totally under the control of the water."

Still another master, Pakuin, wrote: "Zen is nothing but he who asks what Zen is."

These are all phrases that tend to throw attention back upon the state of mind from which the question arose. All these statements are meant to define Zen in one way or another. They are formulations in words not soluble by the human intellect alone—indeed, they are senseless riddles to the rational mind. These statements have both an outer and an inner meaning and because of this they are referred to as kung-an (in Chinese) or ko-an (in Japanese).†

The koans are, then, riddles that are intended to break the logical barrier of thought and throw the mind into the void of intuition. Within this void there is a leap toward life itself, a turning to childhood, yet with the full intellect of a mature adult. Within this intuition we cross the unconscious mind and "see into our own nature."

The koan is only a finger pointing toward the moon. It is intended to synthesize or transcend the dualism of the senses. So long as the mind cannot perceive Hakuin's stream or Basso's haiku, it is limited and divided against itself.

The koans shed light on this duality and help to form a oneness amidst the *all* of man. Within the oneness there can be satisfaction of understanding the nature of one's self.

†Koan in its original meaning pertained to a "case" or an act of law.

The koans, then, are illogical questions and answers. Let me illustrate this.

STUDENT: "I carry many buckets of water each day, master! Now they begin to get heavy."

MASTER: "There is tranquility only in the moon. The water sees it not."

For me to try to explain this would be the reverse of the koan process or, as it might be called, the reverse of the kufu naturalness.

Kufu is naturalness in bodily action, which comes about when the mind allows the body full harmony of its own coordination by not concentrating on a particular part of the body or bodily action. When performing an action the thought of oneness with self-motive† often stands in the way of perfected action. This also relates to koan meditation, for there can be no thought of answering, no thought of achieving in order to achieve.

Zen teaches that the logical mind is a barrier to the process because it restricts one in his degree of perception. Perception can only be achieved when the mind is allowed to act from intuition. To allow logic to yield, the student (shisho) must use illogic or, in short, inspiration. The koan is an intuitive tool for inspiration.

When one has achieved this inspiration he has an openness of mind, a sixth sense. This is why the samurai of old Japan would study Zen so diligently. They began to be able to anticipate an opponent's move. In the act of rapidly drawing their sword (iai), they bridged a void between mind/spirit, heaven/earth and life/death.

Zen Masters (roshi), when they achieved this state of wu-wei (openness), transcended the fear of death. Instead they learned to accept it at every corner, with every breath of air they took in. It

†The self that is expressed here is, of course, the personal build-up picture of the self, or the self-image, not the pure consciousness of the Self. What you are, and what is about you is unique for there is no one or nothing quite the same. We call this the Self. This applies to all things. A piece of stone here appears to be the same as a piece of stone there, the same shape, size and color. But here is here and there is there. The cow in the barn is not the same as the cow in the field. It reflects into others and others reflect into it, each with its own unique oneness and ultimate uniqueness. You are what your response is, but that response is because of your own uniqueness and the uniqueness of the circumstances. This being so, your attempt to see yourself is only part of yourself—namely, a thing of thought, feelings and actions—is bound to lead to a piece of false (incomplete) knowledge, lessening the fullness of life and impeding the response of the whole self to its own environment. And yet, do what you will, even this nonresponse is natural to you, so there is no completely natural response of whole man to whole environment.

is my experience that when one learns not to fear death, the person enjoys life immensely. Fear of death tends to shadow fear of defeat. When there is fear of defeat (in combat, love, business, everyday life) one cannot produce or achieve to one's full potential.

With this advantage of Zen philosophy, the samurai was able to find a "way" that suited his everyday life. It gave him motivation to live that next day, even with the fear of death hanging over his head. It was a philosophy that taught him to enjoy life and not be caught up in the self.

Zen is a way to destroy this fear of death and develop a self-discipline.

The goal of Zen is satori or enlightenment. It is a state of consciousness of the Buddha-mind. Consciousness of pure consciousness itself, as such without objects either mental or physical. It is wisdom or Prajna.

If an experience can be categorized either mentally or emotionally, it is not a satori. In Zen schools satori is seeing into "one's own essential nature," and illuminating the whole of life, but not expressing it.

At the same time it must be said that an intuition may indicate the inner experience of a satori, which for an instant casts its light into the mind, but is destroyed in the process. In the sage's satori, however, the satori casts its illumination and influence in the same way, but is not lost in the process.

In summary, the satori experience can be stated in the phrase: "seeing into one's own nature." This seeing is awakening the consciousness of your conscious.

AN INTERPRETATION OF THE ZEN UNCONSCIOUSNESS

It is an aim of Zen to "wake up the conscious of the unconscious" so an individual can see into his own nature. This seeing is in connection with the center of our being. This center is therefore nothing but the "unconsciousness." Zen's unconscious is thus fundamentally different from the psychologist's unconscious because of its metaphysical overtones.

When Zen speaks of the unconscious in consciousness, it steps beyond psychology: it is not referring even to the unconscious forming the basis of consciousness, which goes to the remotest part where the mind has not yet evolved, the mind still being in the state of mere substance. Nor is the Zen Unconscious a kind of a world-spirit which is found floating on the surface of things. It is timeless, and yet contains all time with the minutest periods as well as all its eons.

To put the Zen Unconsciousness in the most simple terms is to say that it has nothing to do with the unconsciousness that psychology tells us. It is the "original face" of man. By this I am referring to the essence that makes a man before the influence of social norms, that quality that makes him INTUITIVE to his environment, call it enlightenment (satori) or just self-realization.

The unconsciousness in psychology is a sort of storehouse where products of the mind have gone, and may come up again, sometimes with impelling or persistent force, in appropriate circumstances. It has been identified with *lapsed intelligence*, which is similar to the formation of structure in the body, by which every joint and organ, through arising because of a response to environment of the living organism and its resultant adaptation, has become formed and settled by habit. The same process acting somehow in the mind gives us the subconscious, meaning that which has fallen below the threshold of consciousness but is still there in a sort of structure or model form. Instead of calling this "subconsciousness" or lapsed intelligence, it has come to be called unconscious, because it has lapsed below the threshold of consciousness.

In Zen, Unconciousness is conscious of no object including itself. Zen Unconsciousness is the self-nature of man. Thus, when we consider the "self-nature" as direct wisdom of one's Self, we find the key to all our misery within ourselves. This is the truth of Zen; there is nothing more. All is seen and all is content.

If we were to compare the makeup of the mind before a satori, it would look something like this:

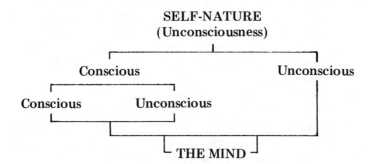

SELF-NATURE
(Unconsciousness)

Conscious   Unconscious

Conscious   Unconscious

THE MIND

When we see into our own nature we are awakening our "unconscious." Not the unconsciousness of Western psychology but the true Self. It is through duality found in society and in its values that the conscious is split into its own conscious and unconscious. This second unconscious (part of conscious) is not the Unconsciousness of Zen. The Unconsciousness of Zen is untouched and needs to be awakened. When there is no duality in the mind, because the person is in contact with his inner being, there is no split and the person is one with himself and thus has gained an inner peace. The mind, after a satori, will look something like this:

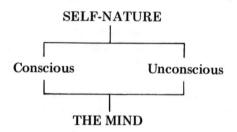

SELF-NATURE

Conscious　　　　　　　**Unconscious**

THE MIND

No duality, no misery, because the person has learned to understand himself. He does away with this split of the conscious, the trickery of the senses, and grasps only the reality of himself. Thus, there is no inner motive that is not known by the consciousness, because the conscious and unconscious are one in the mind.

MUSHIN-NO-SHIN (MIND OF NO-MIND)

Bodhidharma brought with him to China the Indian view that all this world comes from the mind—what we might call the divine mind, since it is beyond all limitations, just as the sun is beyond all clouds. His successors in office up to the fifth patriarch held diverse views under this general idea, but all agreed that meditation should be such as to favor the reception of this pure light without stain or dust. The monk's mind was to be a "mirror bright" and must not gather "dust while it reflects," which means that he must be on guard. It was only upon insight and statement of the sixth patriarch that the doctrine of No-mind came forth. In the meditation of his predecessors the process was one of duality, looking at the pure mind and receiving its light, but Hui-neng insisted that the meditation should be pure seeing, and such pure seeing alone would give truth. It was looking at the reality, and seeing reality that caused the realization of Truth or essence.

* * *

> "The wind blows,
> the bird sings,
> the sound is soundless.
> If you ask me what this
> means, I will say
> I do not
> know."

The poem above holds the essence of the Mushin-no-shin. Let us examine it piece by piece.

The wind and the bird are in simple, light verse. They reflect the object's true nature. The wind does blow, the bird does sing and when each of these objects performs its true nature we feel a thrill of contentment, of expectancy. We feel this expectancy because our mind thrives on it.

Now if the mind is looked at as a black and white thing, an analytical machine, then it is logical and limited. The logical mind sees things that are mathematical, geometrical etcetera. The logical mind does not take chances, it will never step out on a limb. It is straight-laced. It will look at a bird and see only a bird; the bird sings! Why? Because it is expected to sing. If it didn't, the mind would reject that content of thought. The same is true with the wind; if it didn't blow, our logical mind would emit confusion through the body, affecting the endocrine system to the point of stress and nervousness.

Therefore, we can see the logical mind as a strong barrier for the thought process. Perception is the use of an intuitive mind. A person who is perceptive can bring the universe to him or herself and with this perception there is a fuller life. Let us examine the differences:

LOGICAL MIND	INTUITIVE MIND
Bird— Sings	Bird— Peace
Wind— Blows, natural movement	Wind— Complete freedom of movement
Trees— Grow, biological form of living plant matter	Trees— Birth of life in stationary form

This illustrates the difference if one uses logic or intuition. Both have their strong and weak points, but the intuitive mind gives one advantage—anticipation.

Now let us examine the third line of this poem which points directly to the topic, the Mind of No-mind.

A mind conscious of itself is a mind that is not disturbed by affects of any kind. If there is thought, it is not a no-mind. A no-mind keeps nothing in it. It is also called "mushin" or innocent of thought.

When mushin is attained, the mind will flow freely from one object to another, flowing like a stream that fills every possible corner. For this reason the mind fulfills every function required of it. The logic and intuition verge to form one mind, a no-mind.

But when the flowing is stopped at any one point, the result will be a general stiffness and obduracy. The wheel revolves only when the shaft is not too tightly attached to the axle. If the mind has something in it, it will stop functioning and cannot hear; it cannot see, even when sound enters the ear or when light flashes before the eyes. To have something within the mind means that it is preoccupied and has no time for anything else. *But to attempt to remove the thought already fills it with another something.*

The task is endless. It is best, therefore, not to harbor anything. This is what Nan-in refers to when he says, "Empty your cup first, so you can taste my tea." This is difficult, but when you go exercising kufu towards the object, you will after some time come to find this state actualized through each step of progress.

The best description of Mushin-no-shin was written by Yagyu Tajime no Kami, a 17th century swordsman: "The uplifted sword has no will of its own. It is all of emptiness. It is like a flash of lightning. The man who is about to be struck down is also of emptiness and so is the one who wields the sword. None of them is possessed of a mind of any substance. As each of them is of emptiness, the striking man is not a man, the sword is not a sword, and the 'I' that is about to be struck down is like the splitting of spring breeze in a flash of lightning. When the mind does not 'stop' the sword, swinging can be nothing more than the blowing of the wind."[6]

PRAJNA AND DHYANA

The first principle that Hui-neng established about his system of Zen was that, "From the first not a thing is," which self-nature, being not-a-thing, is nothingness. Therefore, seeing into one's nature (self-nature) is seeing into "nothingness." Thus, this seeing is the illumination of the world by the light of prajna. Prajna, then, becomes one of the chief issues in discussing Zen.

Prajna is defined as essential wisdom or awareness of objects or environment and their use and value. Some translate prajna as "Transcendent Wisdom," which means that it transcends the knowledge of things, and also of the mind. This means that prajna is knowing or consciousness or awareness as such, beyond the duality of subject and object. In Zen, prajna is equated to the Buddha-mind, because it is taken to mean Buddha's illumination, and is also equated to the void—void-illumination of body and mind.

To Hui-neng, prajna was essential to satori. But only if the prajna was mixed with dhyana, or actual meditation.

Prajna is in reality one of three subjects of the Buddhist Triple Discipline, which is:

Morality (sila)
Meditation (dhyana)
Wisdom (prajna).

Morality is to observe all the precepts laid down by the Buddha for spiritual welfare of his disciples.

Meditation is the exercise to train oneself in tranquilization, for as long as the mind is not kept under control by means of meditation it is of no use to observe the rules of conduct.

Wisdom or prajna is the power to penetrate into the nature of one's being.

All three are essential for the devoted Buddhist philosopher. Yet when the Buddha died, these three disciplines broke into three separate camps.

The rules set down by the Buddha were used for teachers of the Vinaya. The followers of dhyana were involved in supernatural faculties, such as clairvoyance, mind-reading, telepathy, knowledge of past lives etcetera. Those who perfected prajna were philosophers and intellectual leaders. These separations made the perfection of the Buddhist scriptures impossible. And this was considered a very tragic time for Buddhism.

It was with Hui-neng that some unification took place. To the followers of Shen-hsiu, purification and dust-wiping were essential. Shen-hsiu advocated dhyana first, a stylized tranquilization, and prajna second. Hui-neng in turn unified the dhyana and prajna, but placed special emphasis on prajna; prajna is genuine and dhyana comes along with it.

Hui-neng defined prajna and dhyana as that (dhyana) which is not attached to purity, nor does it (dhyana) concern itself with immovability. What is dhyana then? It is not to be obstructed in anything. Not to have any thoughts stirred up by outside conditions of life, bad or good, this then is dhyana. Outwardly to be free from the notion of form, and inwardly not to be disturbed is dhyana.

When outwardly a man is attached to form, his inner mind is disturbed. But when outwardly he is not attached to form, his mind is not disturbed. Those who find they recognize the outward world, and yet find their mind not disturbed, are in true dhyana.

We now come to prajna, which must be explained in the light of dhyana. There are three concepts that explain the relationship between substance and its function. They are: tai (body), hsiang (form) and yung (use). Body corresponds to substance, Form to appearance and Use to function. The banana is a yellow, long object; this is its form, which appears to the senses. Form belongs to the world of the senses, i.e., appearance. Its Use includes all that it does and stands for, its function (nutrition, to satisfy hunger etcetera). Finally, the Body of the banana is that which constitutes its banana-hood, without which it loses its being, and thus no banana, even with all the appearances and functions ascribed to it. To be a real, full-fledged object, these three values must be present.

To apply these concepts to prajna and dhyana, self-nature is the Body and prajna is its Use. But there is nothing corresponding to Form because the subject does not belong to the world of the senses. There is the Buddha-nature, Hui-neng would argue, which makes up the reason of Buddhahood. This is present in all beings, constituting their self-nature. The object of Zen is to recognize this, and to be released from error, passion. How is this recognition possible? It is possible because self-nature is self-knowledge. The Body is a no-body without its Use, and the Body is its Use. To be itself is to know itself. By using, its being is demonstrated, and this using is, in Hui-neng's definition, "seeing into one's own nature."

This constitutes the difference between the Northern school of Zen called Soto and the Southern school of Zen called Rinzai.[†]

RINZAI AND SOTO ZEN

Zen has two distinct sects in both China and Japan. One, the Rinzai, is the abrupt school founded by Rinzai (died 867), which stresses the philosophy handed down by Hui-neng (prajna and dhyana together, with stress on prajna) and uses the koan as a tool to bring about what is termed "flash enlightenment." The other, Soto, is called the monkish system.

Rinzai tells us to "see" self-nature, which means to wake up the unconscious. Soto in turn tells us to "sit in meditation," so that all our passions and disturbing thoughts may be quieted, and the inherent purity of self-nature shine out of it, by itself.

The teachings of the Rinzai school are fundamentally the Southern school of Hui-neng. In Rinzai, prajna is really a dialectical term denoting that this special process of learning and knowing, known as "abrupt seeing" or "seeing at once," does not follow general rules of logic; for when prajna functions one finds oneself all of a sudden, as if by a miracle, facing Sunyata (emptiness, no-mind). This does not take place with reasoning, but only when reasoning has been abandoned as futile and the willpower is immobilized. This is performed with the aid of the koan. The intellect is wracked against the koan continuously until there is no intellect, only awareness of prajna.

Prajna is pure and unqualified knowledge. It is also often referred to as enlightenment. Prajna is a goal of reasoning.

Rinzai has a fourfold system for snatching away its student's attachments to subjects and objects. They are:

1. Remove the subject and keep the object
2. Remove the object and keep the subject
3. Remove both subject and object
4. Keep both subject and object.

To illustrate this, we have these four statements:

1. "On a warm day the fields are carpeted with flowers; the white of the baby is hanging down like silk." In this there is no subject.

[†]In China they are called Tsao Tung Sect (Soto) and the Lin-Chi Sect (Rinzai). These sects were named after the death of Hui-neng. Hui-neng laid down the foundations of Lin-Chi, and Shen-hsiu those of Tsao-tung, but neither gave a name to the sects which were named by later followers.

2. "Now that the royal writ runs through the land, the commander, free from the smoke of battle, goes abroad." In this there is no object.

3. "Isolation is complete when all communications have been cut." In this there is neither subject nor object.

4. "While the king ascends his precious throne, old peasants sing their song." In this there is both subject and object.[7]

The Soto sect was founded by Sozan and his teacher Tozan.[†] It was taken to Japan by Master Dogen-Zenji in 1227. This sect does not use koans, but follows a method of Mokusho Zen (sitting Zen), including the gentle cross-legged sitting in meditation called zazen.

Training in the Soto school follows a system of Five Stages. These Five Stages are called the Five Relations. These are the relations between a minister and prince, or a host and his guest. Host and prince stand for spiritual reality which is our Real Being and our real home. In contrast with it is the minister or guest, the person who finds himself in this world.

The first stage begins when one discovers or accepts the idea that there is a great spiritual reality, or that there is in oneself some sort of higher or Superior Self very much in contrast to this "little self down here." This Superior Self is called the host or prince, which comes very close to the idea of God or ruler. Philosophically, it is the "real" overshadowing the "seeming," and is represented by a circle in which a large, dark (unseen, unknown) part hangs over a smaller, light (seen) part.

The second stage begins when one realizes that he is a minister, that is, a servant of the prince. He recognizes the spiritual over the material, the spirit as one's master. He discovers that he is only a guest in the world and begins to think that he should act properly towards his host.

He sets aside all desires, personal and worldly, so that he can serve the host better. Philosophically, it is now the overshadowing

†*So*zan and *To*zan put together form the word, SOTO.

or higher and greater principles that are the light, that are the important things, and the man who is dark and foolish, sinful and ignorant. So in the second diagram, the symbol is the same, but the colors are reversed.

In the third stage, the man comes alive, for the real or spiritual now becomes an achievement in the world. There is now positive spiritual living, in place of the old negative responsiveness, which has shrivelled up in the second stage. This is called the upcoming of the real. The servant now feels that the real or higher is himself rather than above or beyond. The guest recognizes more and more the host, so that the host's interests are now the guest's. This is shown with the spirit within the man.

The fourth stage is when the minister or guest becomes more and more luminous with the spirit. This involves an increased wu-wei (openness). Its fulfillment results in constant awareness of reality. This way, wu-wei is not a suppression of mentality, but its decline as motivation, and even as basis of knowledge. The symbol is all light.

Now the guest is in all respects one with the host, or the minister one with the prince, so that there is no other motivation. This will show itself in ordinary life when the man has no longer any planning for his own separate self. This symbol is an all black circle.

Now everything is one, and the realization includes all.

These circles were developed by T'sao Shan. He used a set of horizontal rods, short and long, after the manner of the *I-Ching*.

The five combinations are based on the Tui and Sun trigrams, and the Ta Kuo, Chung Fu and Chung Li hexagrams.

Part Three
Hindu Philosophies

"Even as rivers spring from different sources,
 Yet mingle in the ocean,
 So all the Vedas, all Scriptures,
 All Truth, though of diverse origin,
 Come home to thee!"

     —From the SRIMAD BHAGAVATAM

CHAPTER SIX

"A Fellowship of Faiths"

India has been the stage of intense philosophical activity for many millennia. The Hindu religion of India has shown intense tolerance of all other faiths imported to that country. It has absorbed many ideas and developed into a unique hive of activity. It has passed through a number of stages, three periods, namely:

The Vedic Period (1500—600 B.C.)
The Epic Period (600 B.C. to 200 A.D.)
The Six Systems Period (200 A.D. to present).

The Six Systems that have modernized Hindu philosophy and established it as a world-recognized thought are:

1. The Nyaya System
2. The Vaisesika System
3. The Sankhya System
4. The Purva Mimamsa System
5. Vedanta System
6. The Yoga System

Hinduism has no founder and it has no fixed doctrines or creeds. Yet it does have a number of beliefs held by most Hindus.

The central belief of Hinduism is in one Universal Spirit, or Eternal Essence, without beginning or end, called Brahman, which translates as "World Soul." This World Soul is a three-in-one god because it is believed that Brahman is:

Brahma, the Creator
Vishnu, the Preserver
Shiva, the Destroyer.

These are not separate entities but all come to form one unity.

They all are different manifestations of the same unity. According to this belief, the three gods act in cycles. At the end of such a cycle, called a "Day of Brahman," Shiva destroys the whole world, Brahma creates a new one, and Vishnu appears on the earth in different human forms or incarnations to preserve the world and guide and enlighten man.

Man is considered a part of this eternal World Soul; he consists of a unique mixture of body and soul. The body is like a blanket, an outer garment that one throws away when it is worn out. The soul endures forever. The body is a silly contraption ruled by passions, hate, greed, meaningless ambitions. But the soul, because it is eternal, does not waste its time on meaningless pursuits; instead it is always in the quest for truth.

Archaeologists tell us that as long as five thousand years ago there existed in India a civilization called the Harappa, located around the Indus River.

Then, about 2000 B.C., tribes of the Aryans migrated from Persia and some areas of southern Russia down into the Indus Valley and other northern areas of India.

The word Aryan means "noble." It is believed that from the Aryans came the Rishis, the Sages and Seers who formed most of India's culture. The Rishis were very far advanced in spiritual matters. Their teachings are handed down in the *Upanishads* and the *Vedas.*

As this civilization grew up after the Aryan invasion, certain individuals became expert at various fields. Consequently, a caste system developed.

There is also a mythology that developed, which explained the creation of the caste system. It says that Brahman created the first man, named Manu. Out of Manu's head came the Holy People. Out of Manu's hands came the rulers and warriors. Out of Manu's thighs came the craftsmen of the world. And out of Manu's feet came the rest of the people.

The four castes were:

1. The Brahmins: The Priests and Holy People. Their lives were devoted to the study of sacred scriptures and they were supported by the government.

2. The Kshatriyas: They were the warriors and rulers. They engaged themselves in all kinds of governmental and legal matters.

3. The Vaisyas: The craftsmen, farmers, industrialists. They were merchants.

4. The Sudras: They served the rest of the people. They were workmen, artisans, farm laborers, servants and gardeners. They were not permitted to study the *Vedas*.

Soon there came people who did not even belong to the lowest caste. Although no one precisely knows the origins of the outcasts, it is believed they were a product of intermarriages between separate caste members (strictly forbidden). This category of outcasts was called the "Untouchables."

THE *VEDAS*

The *Vedas* are the sacred scriptures of Hinduism. They are: *Rig-veda; Yajur-veda; Sama-veda; Atharva-veda;* also the *Upanishads*, the *Aranyakas* and the *Brahmanas*.

It is generally accepted that the *Vedas*, or the word Veda, refers to four major books: the *Rig-veda*; the *Yajur-veda*; the *Sama-veda* and the *Atharva-veda*.

The *Rig-veda* is the oldest and most important of the four. The *Rig-veda* is said to have been written "Before the Days of History" and is basically a book of mythology. It consists of over one thousand hymns concerning ceremonial worship and ritualistic rites of devotion. These hymns are arranged into ten books called the *Mandala*. The first six are family books, that is, they were written by sages and poets in the first place and then added to by their descendants. The *Vedas* show clearly the creation of various gods and demi-gods who were important to the early Hindus.

The principle gods in the *Rig-veda* are as follows:

Indra: The main god of the *Vedas* is a hard-hitting, drinking, swaggering warrior who rides his solar chariot across the sky and wields his thunderbolts. As the storm god he brings his rain and moistens the soil for the birth of crops.

Mitra and *Varjuna*: Maintain the cosmic order. Mitra, the sun, presides over friendship and love; Varjuna, the moon, supervises oaths. Like Indra, he is considered a main god.

Both Indra and Varjuna are the heads of the gods. Indra shows his power and is often conceited in his actions. He boasts of his position and intellect. Varjuna (or Varuna), on the other hand, is quiet and makes all his decisions in a peaceful, well-thought-out manner. The two gods represent the two basic qualities that are ingrown in a ruler. A ruler should find the intermediate point between these two.

Agni: The Priests' god of fire, he presides at the altar and the hearth, exists as lightning and blazes at the heart of the sun.

Brihaspati: The god of incantation and ritual, the personification of priestly magic.

Soma: Both a plant and a god who gives inspiration, liberates men and represents the principle of life.

Savitar: The god of motion, and whatever moves or acts depends on this deity with golden eyes, hands and tongues.

Ushas: The beautiful, charming goddess of the dawn, a source of delight to all living creatures.

Puchan: Brings all things into relationship, blessing marriage, providing food, guiding travelers and ushering the dead.

Shiva: The terrifying god of destruction, a deity so formidable that people flatter him to avert his wrath.

Kali: Shiva's empathetic wife, a bloodthirsty fertility goddess decorated with emblems of death.

Pajapati: The master of created beings, the father of the gods and demons and the protector of those who procreate.

Devas and *Asuras*: Gods and demons, respectively, who battle each other with magical powers.

The *Rakshas*: Evil semi-divine creatures who practice black magic and afflict men with misfortune.

Ganesa: A popular god of prosperity, a son of Shiva and Kali, with four arms and the head of an elephant.

The *Yajur-veda* is devoted principally to ritualism. It is written in the form of metrical writing, although at times it has some prose. The *Yajur-veda* concerns itself with sacrifice, priestly functions, ceremonial worship. It concerns itself least with philosophy, metaphysics or spiritual teachings.

The *Sama-veda* is composed mainly of hymns. It is comprised of many verses, melodies and naming of pious exclamatory words which are interjected into singing.

The *Atharva-veda* is the *Veda* of Psychic Power. It gives methods for developing supernormal faculties, senses and powers. There are both low and high methods of getting and using power. The highest is the psychic power, while the lowest is witchcraft, sorcery, black magic or alchemy. There are twenty books in the *Veda* citing various recipes and formulas for blessings, curses, charms, incantations, magical ceremonies, invocations, evocations etcetera. There are two major parts within the *Veda*; they are sections containing Black magic and those containing White.

Brahmanas are commentaries on the *Vedas*, more particularly in the matter of form, ceremonies and creeds, accompanied by numerous references to original Vedic works. From the *Brahmanas* later developed commentaries called *Aranyakas*, or "Forest Commentaries," named after the people who wrote them who dwelled in the forest. The most important of the *Aranyakas* are the *Aitareya* and the *Taittiriya*.

The *Upanishads* form the concluding portion of the *Vedas* and are therefore called *Vedanta* or the end of the *Veda*. Their aim is not so much philosophical *truth* as bringing peace and freedom to the anxious human spirit. They represent free and bold attempts to find out the truth without any thought of a system. Notwithstanding the variety of authorship and the period of time covered by them, a unity of purpose and a vivid sense of spiritual reality may be discerned.

"Upanishad" means "heart-to-heart" instruction. The word is also used to mean an "esoteric doctrine." The *Upanishads* are devoted to theological, philosophical and metaphysical speculation, argument, discussion, teaching and consideration. They are devoted to the consideration of the nature of man and the universe, and the relation to the Infinite Being. The *Upanishads* reach a much higher plane of thought and reasoning than do the earlier works and are nearer to the goals of the philosopher.

The *Upanishads* consist of about 235 sections. The two major *Upanishads* are the *Brihadaranyaka* and the *Chandogya*. In the *Upanishads* are found the complete system of Hindu philosophy and thought, in its many forms and varieties of interpretation. It is the largest collection of philosophical writings in the world. The fundamental principle in the *Upanishads* is the "Inner Teaching."

The *Chandogya Upanishad* gives an account of the gradual evolution of ideas regarding the ultimate basis of things. The seeker tries to find out the one comprehensive principle from which all things are born, by which they are sustained and into which they return at death. His first answer—that matter (annam) is the basic principle—is discarded in view of its inadequacy to explain vital phenomena. The second answer of *life* is found unsatisfactory when sentient entities are considered. The third suggestion of mind (manas) is incapable of accounting for logical phenomena. The fourth formula of logical intelligence (vijnama) cannot be regarded as the highest reality, since there are aspects of being which cannot be reduced to intellectual terms. Thought as ordinarily understood deals with objects viewed as beyond or other than the process of thinking. Reality can be reached in the state of highest immediacy which transcends thought and its distinctions, which is ananda or bliss. Ananda is also the same as Brahman.

The *Brihadaranyaka Upanishad* institutes an inquiry into the nature of the Self. It asserts that the body which is born, grows up, decays and dies cannot be the True Self which persists throughout the changes of birth and death (reincarnation). The True Self is said to be the universal consciousness existing both in itself and for itself. It goes on and offers three states of the soul—waking, dreaming and sleeping—after which it includes a fourth (turiya) which is called intuitional consciousness, where there is no knowledge of objects, internal or external. It is the unchanged identity which continues in the midst of all change. It is the Atman.

Brahman and Atman are one, according to this *Upanishad*. The inmost being of universal nature is the same as our innermost Self.

The morality of the *Upanishads* is in a sense individualistic as it emphasizes self-realization. The term "individualistic," however, ceases to have any exclusive meaning. To realize oneself is to identify oneself with the good that is not private to anyone. Insistence on the knowledge of God (jnana) is tempered by the recognition of the need for moral life.

When the moral striving ends in religious realization the individual is said to be freed from all moral laws. This does not mean that the free can do what they choose with perfect impunity. Laws and regulations are necessary for those who do not naturally conform to the dictates of morality. For those who have risen above the selfish ego and who have died to sin, morality is the very condition of their being.

THE EPICS

The Epic Age of Hinduism (600 B.C.–200 A.D.) saw the writing of two Hindu classics called the *Mahabharata* and the *Ramayana*. To some, this period was known as the "age of philosophical reconstruction."

The *Mahabharata* (begun ca. 500 B.C., added to during many later centuries), the longest poem in the world (about 200,000 lines), is about eight times longer than the Greek *Iliad* and *Odyssey* combined. It is divided into eighteen books. The epic nucleus of the poem concerns itself with the battle between the

Kauravas (Kurus), representing the principle of evil, and the Pandavas (Pandus), representing the principle of good.

The remainder of the *Mahabharata* contains glossaries, descriptions, legends and treatises on religion, law, philosophy and military matters.

The *Mahabharata* contains a full store of mythology and religion of the Hindus.

There are two major works within the *Mahabharata* requiring closer examination. They are the *Bhagavad-gita* and the *Nala and Damayanti*.

The *Bhagavad-gita* consists of only 700 lines but is considered the most important book in Hindu philosophy. It contains a treatise on Yoga, a hymn of praise to Krishna (an incarnation of Vishnu), a section on Bhakti (devotion to God), and the most readable and comprehensive summary of the essential monist doctrines of the *Upanisads*.

The *Bhagavad-gita* introduces three new doctrines to Hindu philosophy:

1. The concept of discontinuous incarnation. Vishnu, in the form of Krishna says, "He who believes in me, when he comes to die, is not reborn, but comes to me."

2. The doctrine of Personal Lord and Master, to whom loving devotion is due. Until this time, the Hindu faith extended to many deities; now it would be confined to one.

3. The theory that life in this world, if lived with detachment from the physical, worldly things, can be a sure way to Nirvana.

The *Bhagavad-gita*, in summary, is the story of the warrior Arjuna who, in order to keep the peace of his nation, has to fight a war with his own brother. Arjuna is troubled and looks to heaven for an answer. The driver of his chariot is Krishna. He gives Arjuna philosophical and religious advice. It is at the end that Krishna shows Arjuna his true form, the incarnation of the Preserver, Vishnu.

Within the text, Arjuna is constantly asking the driver if it is right to kill.

ARJUNA: How can I in battle, shoot with shafts
        On Bhishma, or on Drona—oh, thou chief!
        Both worthy, both honorable men?

KRISHNA: Better to give beggars bread
        With those we love alive,
        Than taste their blood!

ARJUNA: Ah! were it worse—who knows?—to be
        Victor or vanquished here,
    When those confront us angrily
        Whose death leaves us angrily living dread?
    In pity lost, by doubting tossed,
        My thoughts—distracted—turn
    To thee, the Guide I reverence most,
        That I may counsel learn.

KRISHNA: You grieve where grief should not be! You speak
    Words of wisdom, yet you lack all that is wisdom.
    For the wise in heart mourn not for those alive,
                nor for those who die.
    Nor I, nor you, nor any one of these,
    Ever was not, nor ever will be,
    Forever and forever afterwards.
    All that lives, lives anyway, always!
    The spirit and the soul with a strong and constant
             calm
    Take sorrow and joy indifferently,
    Live in the life undying! That which is can never
    Cease to be; that which is not
    Will not exist. To see this truth of both
    Is theirs who part essence from accident,
    Substance from shadow. Indestructible,
    Learn! the life is spreading life through all;
    It cannot by anywhere, by any other means,
    Be anywise diminished, stayed or changed.
    . . . End and beginning are dreams!
    Birthless and deathless and changeless
             remains the spirit forever;
    Death has not touched it at all,
             dead through the house it seems.
    Know me as I am, the very truth.

    Earth, water, flame, air, ether, life and mind
    And individuality—those eight
    Make up the showing of me, Manifest.

    . . . All these hang on me
    As hangs a row of pearls upon a string.

    What Krishna said in this short speech conveyed to Arjuna all the principles that are Hinduism. In this short essay, Krishna summed up the beliefs that still hold.

The *Nala and Damayanti* is a love story concerning conjugal patience and fidelity.

The *Ramayana* (begun ca. 500 B.C., finished ca. 200 A.D.) is a poem of about 96,000 lines, in seven books. It concerns Rama, the perfect king (an incarnation of Vishnu) and his wife Sita. Rama is a prince, the son of King Dasaratha, ruler of the Children of the Sun. Rama's mission on the earth is to save mankind from evil, represented by the ruler of the Giants, King Ravan. It is when Ravan tries to test Sita's faithfulness to Rama that his destruction occurs, leaving the earth clean of evil.

The central philosophy that developed in the Epic Period was that of Materialism. Materialism is called in Sanskrit, lokayata (directing the world), as it holds that only this world is real. According to this philosophy, perception is the only source of knowledge which assumes universal relations. Matter is the only reality, of which the elements are earth, water, fire and air. Consciousness is the function of matter.

There are different opinions about the nature of the soul and it is sometimes identified with the gross body or the senses. There is no future life. As the soul is an attribute of the body, it comes into being when the body is formed by the combinations of the elements. When the body is destroyed, the soul disappears. The world is born of itself. God is a myth we accepted—thanks to our ignorance and incapacity. Pleasure and pain are central facts of life.

The philosophy of Materialism arose to contradict the belief in Krishna and other incarnations of Vishnu. In time, the Materialistic philosophies gave way to the ever-present deity worship.

CHAPTER SEVEN

"The Six Systems"

There are six major systems of Sanskrit philosophy that arose within the time period of 200 A.D. to the present. They are: Nyaya, Vaisesika, Sankhya, Purva Mimamsa, Vedanta and Yoga.

THE NYAYA SYSTEM

The Nyaya system was founded by Gotama sometime during the early Christian Era. The word Nyaya is the Sanskrit word meaning "analysis." Nyaya is a system based on Logic, that truth may be attained by a logical process of examination and analysis. It also contains numerous doctrines concerning metaphysical analysis.

Gotama was a Logician whose system of logic has been justly compared to Aristotle's. Some have gone as far as to call Gotama "the Aristotle of India."

In Greek Philosophy, the syllogism consists of three parts, or propositions, viz., the two premises (or presumed conditions) which form the basis of the argument; and the conclusion, or the result derived from the premises, and which follows them logically.

For example:

> (if)   All men are mortal
> (and if)   Some Indians are men
> (then)   Some Indians are mortal.

The premises are that men are mortal, and that some Indians are men. The logical conclusion to these premises is that "some Indians are mortal."

In the Nyaya system there are five parts or propositions. They are: (a) the Premise; (b) the Proof; (c) the Illustration; (d) the Application of the Proof and (e) the Conclusion.

Nyaya believes that the only way to assert truth logically is through Sixteen Categories or Topics of Discussion (Padarthas, in Sanskrit). These "Topics" are:

1. Means of Knowledge
2. Objects of Inquiry
3. Doubt
4. Purpose
5. Illustrative Precedents
6. Dogma
7. Syllogistic Premise
8. Confutation
9. Ascertainment
10. Discussion
11. Wrangling and Hair-Splitting
12. Caviling
13. Fallacy
14. Prevarication
15. Futile Objections
16. Illogical Argument

A student went through many years of training in these Sixteen Topics until he understood the nature and use of each of them. If he was able to get that far he was able to conduct an examination into the subject of discerning Truth and rejecting Error.

Gotama believed there were four channels of knowledge: (1) Perception through our Senses (pratyaksha); (2) Inference (anumana); (3) Anthology (pupamana) and (4) Testimony of Others (sabda), according to the Laws of Evidence.

Gotama had twelve objects of knowledge:

1. The Soul
2. The Body
3. The Physical Organs of Sense
4. Perception of the Objective World
5. The Higher Consciousness
6. The Mind
7. The Will
8. Error
9. Disembodied Souls
10. Karmic Law

11. Pain

12. The Freedom, Emancipation and Deliverance
of the soul.

Nyaya finds truth in the Atomic theory of the universe. It states that the material world is atomic, and that the souls are countless and become involved and entangled in matter. Liberation can only be attained through the Nyaya system. ". . . Final Beatitudes arise from a proper comprehension of the Truth, as summarized in the Sixteen Padarthas of the Nyaya."

In Nyaya a cause is that which invariably precedes the effect. It is not merely accessory to but is necessary for the production of the effect. Two things cannot be causally related unless there is the positive-negative (anvayavyatrieki) relation between them, such that the presence of the cause means the presence of the effect and vice versa. There are three different kinds of causes:

1. Material (upadana)
2. Nonmaterial (asmavayi) or formal
3. Efficient (nimitta).

The appearance of plurality of causes is traced to defective analysis. When the effect is understood in its uniqueness (karya-visesha), it will be seen to have only one cause.

In Nyaya the individual self is a real substantive being possessing the qualities of knowledge, feeling, desire and aversion. It differs from the body, the senses and the understanding. It is all-pervading though it is not cognizant of many things simultaneously because of differing atomic natures of manas or the "inner senses." It is unique in each individual, and we have an infinite number of souls. The soul is an unconscious principle capable of being qualified by consciousness.

THE VAISESIKA SYSTEM

Sometimes called the "Philosophy of Discrimination," Vaisesika (or Vaisheshika) is formed from the Sanskrit word visheshas, which means "Atomic Individualities." It was founded many centuries before the Christian Era by Kanada.

The Vaisesika Doctrine asserts that after the period of Cosmic Rest, or the Night of Brahman, and at the beginning of the period of Cosmic Activity, or the Day of Brahman (or Day of Brahm), the new universe is begun by the operation of the stored-up Karma or "Essence of Activity" arising from previous universes—energy which has lain dormant throughout the Night of Brahm.

Like other systems, the aim of Vaisesika is to escape the Wheel of Rebirth or Samsara. This deliverance, according to Kanada, is gained by perception of the real soul, and the unreality of matter; and this perception depends upon the knowledge summed up in the Vaisesika Doctrine of the Six Categories.

Kanada based his philosophy upon the fundamental basis of the existence of the Six Categories. They are:

I.   Drava, or Substance. This is described as the "innermost cause of aggregation, collected effect," the fundamental substratum of phenomena, to which all properties and qualities belong, and in which all action occurs. There is a ninefold doctrine attached to Drava:

1. Earth
2. Water
3. Light
4. Air
5. Ether
6. Time
7. Space
8. Soul or Self (Atman)
9. Mind (Manas).

II. Gunas, or Qualities (not to be confused with the Three Gunas or Qualities of the Sankhya philosophy), found in Dravas, or Substance, giving rise to the fine differences in the latter.

Kanada enumerated seventeen Gunas or Qualities:

1. Color
2. Taste
3. Odor
4. Touch
5. Number
6. Dimension
7. Individuality
8. Conjunction
9. Priority
10. Posteriority
11. Understanding
12. Pleasure
13. Pain
14. Desire
15. Aversion

16. Volition
17. Gravity.

Later teachers of this system added seven additional Gunas or Qualities:

18. Disjunction
19. Fluidity
20. Viscidities
21. Sound
22. Merit
23. Demerit
24. Self-Restitution.

It is believed that these qualities are inherent in the soul, and in the substance of matter.

III. Karma, or Action. It is held to consist of Motion only, and to be inherent in and manifested by Substance. It is not the Karma of "Cause and Effect," that is, the doctrine that "to bad goes bad, and to good goes good." This Karma is divided into five motions:

1. Upward Motion
2. Downward Motion
3. Contradiction
4. Expansion
5. Change in Position.

All objective knowledge consists in the perception of things in these three categories, or Padarthas—that is, Drava, Guna and Karma. These three categories are the fundamental universals. The other three are:

IV. Samanya, or Generality, with relation to genus. There are two kinds: (1) Higher and (2) Lower.

V. Vishesha, or Atomic Individuality. The doctrine is that all substance is composed of tiny, invisible particles. It is in the combination of these small particles that we receive all forms of matter, both mental and physical. These Atoms are said to be homogeneous, in that they have the same kind of nature, but are exclusive in nature. They can never blend with each other, but may only form combinations in which the separate atomic individuality of each is preserved.

VI. Samavaya, or Coherence, whereby the parts of certain inseparable things are held together in their respective places.

There was another category added by other teachers which is called Abhava, or nonexistence. This is divided into four classes:

Nonexistence which has a beginning, but no end;
Nonexistence which is without beginning and has no end;
Nonexistence which has a beginning and an end;
Nonexistence which is the negation of identity.

Kanada teaches that understanding is the Quality of the Soul, and that the instruments of understanding are Perception and Inference. He says the Atoms were not created by reason, or a Personal God, but coexist with Him, mingle with Him and are one with Him.

THE SANKHYA SYSTEM

The word Sankhya translates as "Correct Enumeration" or "Perfect Classification." It was founded in 700 B.C. by Kapila.

The basic proposition of the Sankhya system is that there are two active principles in the universe. It is the interaction and interplay between these two active principles that produce the activity of the universe, including that of life and existence. These two principles are: (1) Prakriti, or the primordial substance or energy, from which all matter and energy evolve, and (2) Purusha, or the Spirit Principle, which ensouls or seeks embodiment in Prakriti, and thus gives rise to all forms of variation and difference.

The Sankhya does not posit atoms as the products of matter, instead assuming the existence of countless "spirit atoms" (monads) that compose a Unity.

There are three basic beliefs that separate this system from the others.

I. There is a leaning toward materialism, in that Sankhya refutes the belief in Brahman, and postulates a dual Eternal Thing, one half of the duality being matter. There are two material things, the first is Matter and the second, Spirit, divided into countless atoms. Purusha and Prakriti are immortal, infinite, eternal and self-existent and sustaining.

II. The second belief is that Purusha and Prakriti are "aspects" of the Ultimate Reality. These aspects are eternal and constant, and cannot be withdrawn into Ultimate Reality as emanations may be, but are fixed aspects or "natures" of Ultimate Reality, which always have been and always will be, in periods of activity and nonactivity.

III. The third belief is that both Purusha and Prakriti are

emanations from or "appearances" of Ultimate Reality, but both being finite and destined to pass away in time; that is, to be withdrawn into their common source—Ultimate Reality—at the end of the great period of cosmic rest, which in turn is followed by a period of cosmic activity, and so on.

Like the Vaisesika system, the Sankhya system has various Gunas or Qualities that are needed for the formation of Ultimate Reality. They are:

The Satvas Guna
The Rajas Guna
The Tamas Guna

The Satvas Guna is known as Truth or Harmony. It establishes harmony, wisdom, truth and right action. It is considered imponderable, luminous and agreeable.

The Rajas Guna is known as Passion or Activity. It is the source of physical and mental activity; it sets the mind, the air, the elements and forces of nature into play. It is intermediate between ponderability and its opposite.

The Tamas Guna is known as Indifference or Inertia. It always obstructs, retards, hinders and holds back or endeavors to do so. In its mental aspects it produces ignorance and superstition. It is ponderous, dark and disagreeable.

These three Gunas are the basis of cause in the phenomenal universe in all of its many and constantly changing forms and appearances.

The *Bhagavad-gita* says of these three Gunas that are in conflict with each other, causing the constant changes in the universe: "The fruits of Satvas are called good; the fruits of Rajas are called pain and dissatisfaction; the fruits of Tamas are called ignorance and stupidity. From Satvas is produced wisdom; from Rajas, unrest; from Tamas, foolishness."

The Sankhya holds to the doctrine of Ahamkara, or "Self Consciousness." This doctrine discriminates between the "I" and the "Not-I." The doctrine has three classifications: the Physical, Physiological and Psychological. These three categories are necessary for reality to exist and for the being of man to exist. They are:

I. The Five Tanamatras, or Subtle Elements of Nature, the Ethereal, the Aerial, the Igneous, the Aqueous, the Terrene. From these five elements are produced the five elements of nature: Ether, Air, Fire, Water and Earth.

II. The psychic organism manifests in five senses: Seeing, Hearing, Feeling, Tasting and Smelling. These senses control the Five Instruments of Action: Speech Organs, Hands, Feet, Excretory Organs and the Genitals.

III. The Manas, or mental substance or Energy, manifests itself as the actions of the mind including imagination.

Purusha is the intelligent Self, for whose experience Prakriti evolves. It is a mere witness, a solitary, indifferent spectator. It is the pure consciousness, while Prakriti is unconsciousness. It is inactivity, unalterably constant and devoid of the Gunas, while Prakriti is active, alterable, inconstant and consists of Gunas. Prakriti and its products depend on the light of Purusha, which does not depend on anything else for its illuminations of objects. The Sankhya believes in the plurality of souls and selves. If the self were one, all should become free when one attains freedom, which is naturally not the case. Freedom is not coalescence with the Absolute Spirit but isolation from Prakriti.

The empirical individual is not the pure Self but the self distinguished by the conjunction of the senses etcetera, and limited by the body. While the pure Self remains beyond the intellect, the reflection of the self in it appears as the ego. Activity belongs to the intellect, and on account of its union with Purusha the indifferent Self appears as an actor. Though not an agent, the Self appears as an agent through confusion with the agency of nature, even as the latter through proximity to the Self appears to be conscious. Every ego possesses within the gross material body, which suffers dissolution, a subtle body formed of the psychical apparatus including the senses. This subtle body is the basis of rebirth as well as the principle of identity throughout various existences.

The evolution of nature is adapted to the ends of the Self. The spiritual centers are, however, incapable of exerting any direct influence on nature, though they are said to excite it to activity. The union of Self and nature is compared to a lame man of good vision mounted on the shoulders of a blind man of sure foot.

PURVA MIMAMSA SYSTEM

The term Purva Mimamsa comes from two Sanskrit words; the first, "Purva," meaning "prior, former or previous;" the second, "Mimamsa," meaning "investigation, research or examination." It is used to oppose the term Uttara Mimamsa or "subsequent or final examination." It is the orthodox organization of the six philosophical systems implied in its name.

This system uses the original texts and beliefs of the early Hindu systems, the *Vedas* particularly. They claim divine inspiration for the *Vedas* of India, and claim their philosophy is based on the ancient interpretation of these books.

While the majority of the Hindu philosophies proudly boast that they are not "religiously founded upon a book," Purva Mimamsa boasts it is founded as such. Most of the Hindu philosophies claim they are based on pure reason. While they take pleasure in showing that their teachings are supported by passages in the *Vedas*, they do not claim their systems of thought to be founded on them. Purva Mimamsa does not claim to be based on truth or reason, but instead on the pure interpretation of the *Vedas*. Being so based, it claims to be the pure and true form of thought.

Jaimini founded this school, or rather collected the texts and adopted the name.

This system has a large following and was responsible for the preservation of the Vedic myths, beliefs and doctrines.

THE VEDANTA SYSTEM

The Vedanta school has the greatest following in and out of India. At the present time it is considered the leading and most important of the systems.

Vedanta is also called Uttara Mimamsa or the "final examination" or "the investigation of the later part." It is in opposition to Purva Mimamsa or "prior investigation."

"Purva" refers to the study of the first part of the *Vedas*, or the ritualistic and ceremonial parts.

"Uttara" relates to the date of the founding of the school (after the Purva Mimamsa) and to the study of the later parts of the *Vedas*, known as the *Upanishads*.

Vedanta then has come to mean, "the last part of the *Vedas*."

Most philosophers assert the founding of this system in 700 B.C. under the direction of the sage, Badarayana. Others claim the direct founding by the deity, Vyasa.

The Vedanta has two doctrines; that is, an outer doctrine and an inner doctrine—the outer, or rather several outer ones, being for the masses who are not able to grasp the high conception of the inner doctrine which is for those few individuals with the philosophical capability to grasp Absolute Idealism.

The inner doctrine concerns itself with investigations into Brahman, or the Absolute, and the manifestations of Brahman as the phenomenal universe with its individual souls.

The Vedanta fathers founded the doctrine of THAT, the Absolute, Brahman. Firmly established in the Hindu mind, the ONE or THAT was recognized as the source of ALL—or the ALL itself.

While other systems of Hindu philosophy assert that there is a dual aspect to THAT (e.g., Sankhya philosophy holds to the dual aspect of manifestations, viz., a. the innumerable individual souls or Purusha; b. the Prakriti, or Nature, which supplied the material), Vedanta embraces the concept of Monistic Idealism, which holds that the One is the only Reality, and that consequently all else that appears to exist must be illusory, or an appearance of the One as Many, without an actual separation of the One into parts.

Therefore, the One is the Brahman or the THAT. This being so, the term "manifestation" must be abandoned, and the term "reflection" or "appearance" substituted. The One is indivisible and incapable of separation; therefore, there can be no manifestations, only illusions, reflections and appearances.

Thus, anything outside the One must be merely ideas, or existing thoughts of this One. With this concept the Vedanta system brushed all existing ideas away, leaving a clear doctrine of THAT: "Any other aspects or principles are merely ideas in the mind of the One." They are Maya (illusion).

The most important thing to consider in the discussion of Vedanta is the Doctrine of the One.

The One is held to be beyond the qualities or attributes; beyond subject and object; to be the *source of being*; Intelligence; Bliss. It is the efficient cause of the universe in its spiritual, mental and material appearances; creator and creation; doer and deed; cause and effect; the Underlying Truth amidst the Universe of Unreality; One; Self-Existence; all-there-is; all-that-ever-was; Only and Only; all-that-ever-can-be, without a second.

The souls of men are only reflections of the Absolute, which take shape within our own world (also an appearance of the One). The soul has several "principles" or "sheaths:"

> Rupa or Physical Body
> The Jiva or Prana or Vital Force

(Ch'i, in Chinese)
The Linga Sharira or Astral Body
The Kama Rupa or Animal Soul
The Manas or Human Soul
The Buddhi or Spiritual Soul
The Atman or Spirit

One final thing to mention about Vedanta is that the followers believe in all knowledge as part of the One. Being so, knowledge has taken on a religious significance for them. Badarayana once said, "Wisdom is the only good." Thus, the perfect way to live is the way centered around Gnani, or Knowledge.

In summary, Wisdom is the path favored by the Vedantist, which consists in the understanding of the great underlying Truths concerning THAT and the Universe, and which is also a favored path of the Sankhyas and of the Vaisesikas—the Vedantists paying more attention to the understanding of the Universe in its phases of Soul and Substance. The Sankhya devotes more consideration to the question of how in the phenomenal world and the universal life than to the subject of THAT in the abstract universe; the Vaisesika system, only in terms of the abstract. Nyaya with its logic is completely abstract, yet it is considered logical because the existence of the One is illustrated and proved, not just taken for granted.

Thus, each system has its strong and weak points, each contributing something in the way of completeness, not just for themselves, but for the Oneness of Hindu philosophy.

CHAPTER EIGHT

"Yogic Philosophy"

The word yoga comes from the Sanskrit word, "Yuj," which means "to join" or "to yoke." This leads to the definition of yoking two things together or joining one thing to another.

In times long past, Sanskrit was considered a secret language taught only to priests and neophytes of high caste. It was handed down from mouth to mouth by the guru (master or teacher) and the chela (student).

Yoga itself has many definitions and many interpretations of the "yoking" process. Let us consider some of them.

Union or method of union

Any outside thing united to another outside thing

The mixing of one thing with another as sugar to water

The uniting of cause with effect as with sparks and the fire producing them

A method of keeping things in their proper place

A symbolism with an inner meaning, like a code or a proverb

To hide one thing and try to show another as a conjurer would do, or to signify a thing without telling it as a hint

Different significance in words which vary according to different minds

Physical exercise

Proper composition of language to convey description

Any skill or dexterity

Method to protect one's possessions: physical, mental or spiritual

To find means of acquiring things by deep contemplation

Conversion of one substance to another, as in Chemistry

To unite souls (two) for any purpose

To produce a current of thought for a specific attainment

To suspend all activity and to concentrate the heart upon one particular thing.[8]

There are various schools of thought to yoga. Each approaches the goal of Nirvana differently. They are:

School of Yoga	Gain Mastery Over	Control Over
(1) HATHA	Breath	Physical Body and Vitality
(2) LAYA	Will	Power of the Mind
(a) Bhakti	Love	Power of Devotion
(b) Shakti	Energy	Power over Energizing Forces of Nature
(c) Mantra	Sound	Power of Sound Vibrations
(d) Tantra	Form	Power of Geometric Shapes
(3) DHYANA	Thought	Power of Thought Process
(4) RAJA	Method	Power of Discrimination
(a) Jnana (Gnani)	Knowledge	Power of Intellect
(b) Karma	Activity	Power of Action
(c) Kundalini	Kundalini	Power of Psychic and Nerve Forces
(d) Samadhi	Self	Power of Ecstasy[9]

Of these twelve systems, five are considered essentially important and will be looked at more deeply. I am referring to: (a) Hatha Yoga, for general development of physical fitness and health; (b) Karma Yoga, yoga of cause and effect, of action; (c) Bhakti Yoga, yoga of devotion, prayers toward God; (d) Raja Yoga, for improvement of mental powers; (3) Jnana (Gnani) Yoga, for seekers of true knowledge.

Yogic philosophy in general looks at the body as being made up of seven parts or principles:

    1. Physical Body — gross material body
    2. Astral or Etheric Body — invisible
    3. Absolute Energy, Vital Force, or Prana
    4. Instinctive Mind
    5. Intellectual Mind
    6. Spiritual Mind
    7. Spirit.

The physical body itself is made up of various chemicals, creating what might be called the Human Shell. Within the human shell there are: 10 gallons of water, enough fat to make seven bars of soap, enough carbon to make several thousand pencils, enough phosphorous to make 2,000 matches, enough iron to make a three-inch nail, enough lime to whitewash a small hencoop, with additional small amounts of magnesium and sulphur.

This then is the physical body, an organism made for the sole purpose of containing the other six qualities, namely the Spirit. Because of its limited use, to dwell on the physical body is a waste of time.

The Astral body is still a material thing, but is invisible to the human eye. Yogis and clairvoyants are said to be able to see the Astral plane. The Astral body is an exact counterpart of the physical body and is connected by a thin thread. When we die this thin thread is broken and the Astral body leaves the physical body and in time disintegrates in the normal physical dissolution.

The Astral body has no intelligence of its own, but is the seat of all our desires, our animal passions and our lower emotions. When one is advanced, it is possible to have intelligence in the Astral body, allowing it to roam within the Plane, manifesting knowledge. The nearest comparison to the Astral body is the existence of ice, steam and water. Each receiving temperature stimulae advances to a higher state, ice to water, water to steam. The steam is invisible but contains all the elements, and in this sense, is ice. So too, the Astral body, when trained, is invisible, but contains all the intelligence of the physical body.

The third principle is called Absolute Energy or Prana. It comes from the Sanskrit word meaning "breath." Thus, Prana is the breath of life. It is an intrinsic life energy that dwells within and without our bodies. When we take in food we are absorbing Prana, some foods containing more Prana than others. Foods that are exposed to light and natural sources contain more energy of Prana than those growing underground.

The force of Prana may be called life itself, for without Prana life cannot exist. When absorbed within our bodies, it flows like a stream, granting energy to each and every cell. From without, it gives to nature and the universe.

The fourth principle is called the "Instinctive Mind." We now move out of the lower plane of physical existence and move to the intermediate, that is, the Mental.

All work carried on by the body under the plane of consciousness is performed by the Instinctive Mind.

All forms of matter contain an Instinctive Mind, including the
rocks and minerals. This can be seen in crystal formations of
rocks. The basic crystal is able to grow, to split and to reproduce
itself, reproducing other crystal forms identical to each other. Each
mineral and rock has its own invariable form or pattern, indicating
that this is no accident, but it is the law that like produces like.

The Instinctive Mind produces these likes; it is the pattern of
life. The Instinctive Mind controls this high level of production
and the low level of unconscious organ movement within the
Human Shell. These movements do not require thought, but act
naturally because they are the pattern of the organism, thus the
fundamental duty of the patterning force, the Instinctive Mind.

The level right above the Instinctive Mind is the Intellectual
Mind. These two form the intellect of the individual, in a single
term, the MIND.

The intellect is the level that separates us from the lower class
of animals. Up to this point we share in common all the levels as
does a snake or ant. Each of these creatures has a Physical Body,
an Astral Body, Prana Energy and an Instinctive Mind. The only
element they are lacking is the Intellectual Mind, the intellect.
This is the important key that separates the human from the
animals, the process of thought and reasoning.

The Spiritual Mind is beyond the realms of normal human
conditions and human consciousness, and is the source of all our
higher thoughts, ideas, aspirations, inspirations, self-sacrifice,
devotion, all those aspects and qualities which are highest and best
in man. It is sometimes referred to as: the "Over Soul" or the
"Superconsciousness Mind."

The last level and principle is the Spirit. Because few have really
ever reached this state of being, there is little that can be said of it
other than that it is the pinnacle, the goal. It is called the "Light
of God, the God of Love."

The *Yoga Sutras* (Scriptures of Yoga) give "Eight Limbs,"
which have been designated to assist the chela on the Path of
Nirvana through Yoga. These "Eight Limbs" are steps to the final
stage, Samadhi or the union with the Spirit. They are:

1. Yamas, or abstentions
2. Niyamas, or observances
3. Asanas, postures and exercises (as in Hatha)

4. Pranayama, breath control
5. Pratyahara, or the withdrawal of senses
6. Dharana, act of concentration
7. Dhyana, meditation
8. Samadhi, spiritual or superconsciousness.

The Yamas are divided into ten rules, often referred to in Yoga as the Ten Rules of Conduct:

Noninjuring of others, either physically or mentally
Truth and discernment in all things
Nonstealing and respect of others' property
Observances of continence and chastity
Practice of forgiveness, tolerance and understanding
Endurance, forbearance and obedience
Compassion and sympathy
Sincerity and earnest endeavor
Proper control of diet in quality and quantity
Practice of hygiene and purity, both physical and mental.

The second limb on the "Eight Limbs of Samadhi" is called the Niyamas or Rules of Conduct. Niyama is broken down into Ten Rules as follows:

Penance and retribution for wrongdoing
Acceptance and contentment
Faith
Charity and nongossip
Veneration of holy things and adoration of God
Study of sacred scriptures, attending discussions on sacred subjects
Modesty and simplicity
Development of mental qualities and mental pursuits
Prayer and meditation
Unselfish actions, self-sacrifice and help to others.

The obstacles to Yoga (and therefore Spiritual Advancement) are, according to the Yoga Scriptures, as follows:

1. Sensual pleasures of *all* description—the sexual pleasure eats up the Prana and thus takes essential energy away that should be used for meditation
2. Violence, hatred and all kindred emotions
3. Lust for power
4. Ignorance

5. Egotism and snobbery
6. Envy and jealousy.

* * *

Color	Seen Issuing From	Interpretation
Yellow (Bright)	Around the head	Indicates high spiritual advancement and a highly intellectual individual. Said to be protected from infections.
A Rose Crimson	Within the chest	Deep affection. A feeling of love in the highest sense causes the Aura to pick up a crimson glow.
Dull, Heavy Crimson	Within the forehead	Represents lust and sexual love.
Blue	Within the head, middle of forehead, within or around chest, or a general glow around the body.	Represents religious emotion, also a pure individual.
Black	Around the head	Hatred or malice.
Green	General glow around the body or from the head.	Jealousy and deceit.
Grey	The middle of the forehead or chest area.	Melancholy.
Violet	Head area	Mental purification.
Amethyst	General bodily glow	Refinement.
Emerald Green	Within the chest, or head area.	Happy circumstances and good fortune.
Turquoise	General bodily glow	Relaxation, calmness of nerves.

When the seven principles of man are in connection with each other, they form the HUMAN AURA. Each of these seven principles of man gives off separate vibrations. It is the sum of these vibrations that forms the colorful halo around our bodies (either centered around the head or from the chest). The Aura, by the color it holds, gives a complete makeup of the attitude of an individual. A person who has trained for any length of time in any form of yoga will in time develop an acuteness of sense and an empathy towards life and the Spirit. What this means is that the yogi will be able to sense and *see* various colors given off by the individual. These colors represent a particular mood.

Colors are seen in a variety of places on the body and in varying degrees of density. Therefore, a complete explanation of all the colors and their meaning would be a much too complicated task. It might even require a separate volume. However, I have discussed the basic and most central colors.

Yoga gives a fourfold aim in search of the Spirit. They may be called signposts directing us on the way. They are:

1. DHARMA—Be faithful to the natural and ethical laws of the country and community. Be faithful to your lot in life. Thus, it can be called the faithfulness of *Man's Duty*.

2. ARTHA—This is securing one's financial position in life. This way, one's mind is clear and without tension on the Path of Enlightenment.

3. KAMA—Have the right kind of ambitions, desires and a good guru.

4. MOKSHA—This teaches liberation from fear and ignorance by having knowledge of yoga. It teaches detachment from material things and pleasure of the senses. Thus being liberated, the mind is free to rise to higher planes.

HATHA YOGA

Hatha Yoga is the science of bodily care and good health, also concerning itself with the purification of both body and mind.

This purification and perfection are accomplished by performance of various postures referred to as Asanas.

There are six principal exercises which the yogi is required to carry out according to the classical text of Yoga. These are called the "Six Kriyas," which can be translated as "Six Duties" or "Six Actions." They are:

1. Dhauti—to clean and purify the mouth and throat

2. Neti—cleaning of the eye by concentrated gazing (usually with a candle)
3. Trataka—cleansing the nasal passages by means of catheter or similar instrument
4. Bhasthi—cleansing the bowels and intestines by flushing (by salt water)
5. Nauli—cleansing the bowels and intestines by muscular control only
6. Kapala Bhati—purification by breathing.

These six exercises are for the purpose of granting good health and long life. These six purification exercises are performed along with the Asanas (postures) for health to clear the path on the spine for the Kundalini force to flow.

Kundalini is a force that sleeps at the base of the spine. The Kundalini must pass through channels called Chakras. The Chakras are said to look like little lotus flowers and are located along the spine. The six Chakras are as follows:

1. Mulandhara, at the base of spine, near the anus.
2. Swadhisthana, at the level of the genital organs.
3. Manipuraka, at the level of the navel.
4. Anahata, at the level of the heart.
5. Anahata Vishuddi, at the level of the throat.
6. Ajna, at the level of the eyebrow.

The Yogic exercises found in Hatha Yoga help to clear away the "dust of time" from these Chakras so that the Kundalini (looking something like a coiled snake) will flow through these channels. When it reaches the top (the Ajna), the student has gained Samadhi.

The Asanas are sometimes attributed to Patanjali, called the "Father of Yoga" (2nd Century B.C.). With modern scholarship, we have found that Patanjali was not the founder, rather the codifier of the Yogic philosophy and methods of practice. He authored the *Yoga Sutras*, four books dealing with contemplation (Samadhi), the practice of yoga, the psychic powers and liberation from Samsara.

The characteristics of the Asanas as compared to Western exercises are that the Asanas are effortless, relaxing and energy-giving, contrasted to Westerners' exercises being effortful, nerve-binding and energy-sapping. To the Westerner, to be physically fit means to have big, bulging muscles, whereas to the yogi, physical fitness means having all the *organs* in tune with themselves and operating in tip-top shape.

The Asanas are performed slowly, trying to hold them for as long as possible. While in these twisted postures, you perform pranayana or breathing exercises.

The characteristic about these breathing exercises is that they are performed with the abdomen and diaphragm. Patanjali once said, "You live as you breathe," meaning that all life is centered around the consumption of breath, and the better consumed, the longer the life.

The word Hatha comes from two Sanskrit words conveying the breathing principles. "Ha" is taken to mean the action of inbreathing, the "tha" is taken to mean the outbreathing. They are called, therefore, the Sun (Ha) and the Moon (Tha) breaths.

Thus, from the name, we can see the chief purpose of Hatha Yoga—that is, to control your breathing process and secondly, to master the physical body (health and purification of the Chakras).

KARMA YOGA

Since the human organism in itself is geared for work by the very formation of muscle and bone structure, it would seem natural that a Yoga would be devised in order to utilize this function. Karma Yoga is such a system.

Karma Yoga is the Yoga of Action or work. If work is done for achievement of personal desires or selfish goals, then it is not Karma Yoga; in turn, if the desires and works are for the betterment of others, or the "welfare of the world," then it is Karma Yoga.

The industrialist who takes into account the welfare of his customers, employees, associates and all whom he deals with or meets in the course of his commerce is a Karma Yogi.

The same concept applies in all walks of life, in all fields of business. It makes no difference if the person is in contact with one person or a million persons; thus, all can be Karma Yogis if they are unselfish in their ways.

The subject of Karma Yoga was spoken of at great length by Krishna in the book, the *Bhagavad-gita*. It says that action should be motivated by knowledge and love, of mind and soul. With this in mind we can recall the definitions given earlier about Bhakti and Jnana Yoga (devotion and knowledge, respectively). We can see therefore that Karma Yoga is a complement to other systems.

It is an outlook and a doing, more than it is a theory.

When Karma Yoga mixes with Bhakti, there is a working towards and for God. There is self-sacrifice for the world, so that the yogi can be considered a servant of God, not just someone preaching his principles. A life is spent in areas where his help will be the betterment of the community. This way, the community will see this man as such a servant; thus the Karma becomes a catalyst for converting more followers to the way of God.

When Karma mixes with Jnana (knowledge seeker, philosopher), there is no duality between God and man, thus the seeker sees the Infinite Being at the center of himself. There is a personal heaven. The secret of the Jnana approach to work consists in discrimination. Specifically, it consists in drawing a sharp line between the empirical self, immersed in action, and the Eternal Self which stands aloof from it. Man's usual interest in work relates to the consequences it will have for the empirical self, the pay or acclaim it will bring. This is the selfish, egotistical way, that leads nowhere except to mistrust and dissatisfaction. The Karma Yogi leads his spirit to complete detachment, almost dissociated from the empirical self. Identifying himself securely with the Whole or Eternal, the worker goes about his duties but as these are being effected by his empirical self, his True Self is in no way evolving with him. It is when he can break this influence by unselfishness that the True Self evolves. Karma Yoga aids in this breaking because the goal is not materialistic or egotistical, but world benefiting. Thus, the True Self develops, and the person being controlled by his True Self can give more in the way of benefit to mankind.

BHAKTI YOGA

Bhakti Yoga is the way to Nirvana through Love. It is the way to see God, not as something within ourselves, but as something without, and the only way to be part of Him is to love Him.

All the basic principles of Bhakti are those of Christianity, that loving devotion towards God brings peace. Differing from Jnana Yoga which sees God within the person, Bhakti Yoga stresses a dualistic conception between God and man. To the Bhakti Yogis, God is more than the mind; instead, it is a deity requiring love.

Bhakti rejects all suggestions that the God he loves is himself, even his deepest self, and insists instead on His otherness. The Bhakti Yogi wonders how anyone can conceive God as himself. He says that he "wants to taste sugar, not be sugar."

Also, according to the *Song of Tukaram*, a Hindu classic:

Can water quaff itself?
Can trees taste the fruit they bear?
He who worships God must stand distinct from him,
So only shall he know the joyful love of God;
For it is said that God and he are one,
This is wrong, for if it were so,
All that joy, that love, should vanish instantly away.

Pray no more for utter oneness with God:
Where were the beauty if jewel and setting were one?
The heat and shade are two,
If not, where were the comfort of shade?
Mother and child are two,
If not, where were love?
When after long being shuttered, they meet,
What joy do they feel, the mother and child!
Where were the joy, if the two were one?
Pray, then, no more utter oneness with God.[10]

The Bhakti Yogi thus adores God with every element of his being.

This great love embraces the follower and enables the yogi to live a fuller, happier life, with greater meaning and significance. For his love of God will reflect in everything he does and will bring him closer to enlightenment.

This God of the yogi can be many things, and in the course of Hindu religious philosophy it indeed represented a multitude of deities. Brahman, Krishna, Kali and Indra are just a few. In fact, the term "God" can represent anything, the Christian Triad (Father, Son and Holy Spirit), or even Buddha.

RAJA YOGA

The word Raja comes from the Sanskrit word meaning "Royal." It is the Royal system of Yoga. It asserts that man himself is the king of all his mental and physical possessions and powers. It aims at his mental and bodily realization of his status as master, and ultimately his status of complete nondependence on anything outside himself. Thus it is in complete contradiction to the Bhakti system.

This being so, the Raja Yogi does not allow that bodily

practices can generate or improve mental powers and insights, though he agrees that they can lessen or remove certain obstacles and hindrances due to their own defect or defects induced in them by wrong thinking and actions of the past.

For this reason, Raja Yoga supports a system of quietistic meditation, where the chela sits in meditation to still his being. In this way, he can wipe away all his hindrances of submerged events.

The Raja Yogi does not study any scriptures or dogmas, for everything is within himself and all he has to do is learn to draw it out.

The Raja Yogi looks at the human being as a stratified man. There are four basic layers. The first is the body; this is the shell we carry ourselves in day after day. The second is the part of being that he is aware of, the mind and its conscious personality. Underlying these two is the third layer, the realm of his individual subconsciousness. This has been built up by his past life experiences down through the years. Although it cannot be seen, it shapes the personality and the actions that we perform in the normal daily hours. These three views are parallel to the Western view of the mind. The fourth layer underlying the other three is Being itself.

It is the Raja Yogi who makes use of the Eight Limbs (as discussed at the beginning of this chapter) of Yoga. These Eight Limbs help break through the top three layers in order to allow the fourth layer, the True Self, to shine through. When the yogi has reached the Eighth Limb (Samadhi), he will not only have reached enlightenment, but also the realization of himself as the master, and the ability to prove it.

JNANA (GNANI) YOGA

Jnana Yoga translates as the "Way of Knowledge." It is a system geared toward the philosopher and the thinker.

Jnana Yoga asserts that the guiding image of the infinite sea of being, underlying the tiny waves of our finite self, is our makeup. God is the all-pervading Self, as fully present within us as He is without. The task then is to recognize our identity with Him. God is then impersonal, for the characteristic of ultimate reality that most impresses the philosopher is His infinitude, which, in comparison to personality, embodying as it does certain properties to the exclusion of others, must always seem, in some respects, finite and limited.

In this way, the Jnana Yogi sees God within himself. He does not believe himself the master of the universe as does the Raja Yogi, nor does he feel that God controls everything as does the Bhakti Yogi. He feels that God is present within himself, and his task is to learn to understand this presence and allow God to work through him.

The goal of the Jnana Yogi is to cleave the domain of ignorance with the blade of discrimination. This is to distinguish between the surface self and the Real Self. There are three steps on the Path which must be followed in order to achieve this discrimination.

They are:

1. HEARING: the aspirant (student) listens to various scriptures and philosophical dissertations to acquaint himself with the knowledge that there lies at the center of his being the infinite unthwartable fount of being itself.

2. THINKING: This process is the actual thought pattern the student will choose in order to arrive at this realization. Sometimes the master will tell the student to examine the language he uses in his everyday life. Look at the word "my." You talk of "my book" or "my pencil." You are referring to possessions, not parts of you, but when you talk about my soul or my belief or even my being, you are talking of things that are part of you, those things that you cannot separate from the Real Self.

The master tries to evoke images for the student that will help him come to this realization. In time, the True Self will break through because the surface self and the True Self are like oil and water; they cannot mix by themselves, they need constant mixing, and even in the mixture, the oil will show through. This is true with the two selves. Although they will mix, the True Self will always stand out.

3. SHIFTING AND SELF-IDENTIFICATION: The student now must meditate on his identification with the Infinite Being, trying to think of himself as such even while going through everyday tasks. The yogi at this point is looking at himself in the third person. Instead of saying, "I am walking down the street," he says that "Smith (referring to himself) is walking down the street." Everything is looked at as separate from the Eternal Self.

If the person feels pain, it is the body feeling pain, not the True Self. With practice, this third step produces complete detachment and allows the person to look at himself as being the storehouse of the True Self, making the True Self and the surface self, one.

BRIEF DEFINITIONS OF OTHER YOGA SYSTEMS

MANTRA YOGA: Makes use of sounds for stimulation of the senses. The yogi applies Mantras or chants that have certain vibrations, to induce the required mental state. They are words and sentences that are continually repeated, creating rhythm to which certain senses respond. In some cases the effect is hypnotic. In Tibet, for example, the monks chant repetitions of a phrase (e.g., Om mani padme hum) together with dim lighting and the use of incense, inducing a trance-like state. In other cases, it is the content of the phrase that counts. For example, if you chant "All is Good" enough, it is believed that you will agree that all is good.

SHAKTI YOGA: The Yoga that studies the fundamental powers or forces found in the universe. These sources originated from the source of all being, the Brahman or Absolute.

The Shaktis believe they can channel these forces into Chakras of the body, granting them supernatural powers.

Popularly, the powers which come about at various stages of yoga practice are:

1. Jnanashakti—perceptive faculties: clairvoyance, telepathy, psychometry and even reading of tea leaves, crystals, embers and clouds.

2. Kriyashakti—concentrated thought-picturing without thought-activity, but within the background, a material intention to change or manifest something.

3. Ichchhashakti—willpower, which is needed for self-control, leading to abnormal controls of the body, astral projection etcetera.

4. Mantrashakti—Power of sound or rhythm, vocal expression or music. Used in rainmaking and other stimulations of nature.

TANTRA YOGA: A system containing many formulas for the worship of deities, which are symbolic, with a view to the use of power. It is therefore somewhat mechanically magical. They use various symbols and geometric shapes to bring about this deity-summoning. When the deity appears, they take great pains in controlling it for powers. The word Tantra means "loom."

LAYA YOGA: A system of yoga in which the chief emphasis is upon the awakening of the Kundalini force, which sleeps as a coiled snake at the base of the spine. Closely linked with this are the scriptures of the Tantra sect, which contain mystical formulas to summon gods and goddesses to help awaken the Kundalini within oneself.

OTHER HINDU PHILOSOPHIES

JAINISM

Although Jainism had a crucial influence in transforming Hinduism, there are only about two million followers in India today. Yet the number of Jains is disproportionate to the impact of this unique religion and philosophy on both Hinduism and the culture of India. Jains are followers of Jinas, persons who have attained immortality and happiness by righteous thoughts and deeds. A Jina is someone who preaches Jainism and is known as a Tirthankara. There were twenty-four Tirthankara. The first was Shri Adinath, who lived about 800 B.C. and attained enlightenment in 772 B.C., when he named himself Parsva.

Contemporary Jains follow the 24th Tirthankara, Mahavira (500 B.C.), who flourished around the same time as Buddha. He was born of the Kshatriya caste; his parents strictly worshiped Parsva. Mahavira married and fathered a daughter; but in his thirtieth year, when his parents died, he asked his guardian and brother, Nandivradhana, to allow him to become a monk. After receiving his permission, Mahavira spent the next twelve years wandering through the forest, practicing denial and becoming a nudist. At seventy-two, he obtained release from the dreaded Hindu fate of reincarnation, proving that such a release was possible for men and women who were not Brahmins. Mahavira died a suicide, using a method that became an example for later followers: self-induced starvation, a symbol of his oneness with life, including plants.

Ahimsa (nonviolence) is not just the foundation of Jainism but a daily principle for every thought and deed. There are five strict principles that the Jain monk must follow, which are also guidelines for the lay Jains:

1. Ahimsa—to avoid all killing; thus the Jain must walk carefully to prevent destroying unseen creatures.
2. Asatya Tyaga—never to lie, be greedy, or lose one's temper etcetera.
3. Asetya Varata—never accept what is not given.
4. Brahmacharya—to practice celibacy and chastity.
5. Aparigraha Varata—to avoid attachment to any living or dead objects.

Because of their deep belief in Ahimsa, lay Jains for centuries have consistently made their living in certain professions since they are unable to have any connection with agriculture, butchery, fishing or brewing. As a result, their careers have been limited to business and therefore the Jains in India are on the whole far more successful and prosperous than the Hindu majority.

Jainism, as a religion, is considered a heretical belief because it does not recognize the authority of the Vedic Scriptures. Furthermore, Jains do not believe in one God but that God is within each man. Strict asceticism is recommended as a means to finding the God within.

A Jain layman must go through two preliminary stages if he is to follow the Jain principles. They are:

1. Faith in Jainism through studying the doctrines and believing in them.
2. Becoming a Pakshika Sravaka, layman intent on following the path of salvation. There are twelve duties involved:
   A. To have faith in Jainism
   B. To abstain from intoxicants
   C. To abstain from flesh foods
   D. To abstain from fruits that would contain insects; to abstain from honey
   E. To abstain from taking four kinds of food at night: edible, tastable, lickable and drinkable
   F. To drink clean, filtered water
   G. To abstain from gambling
   H. To follow the five guidelines
   I. To abstain from hunting
   J. To abstain from adultery
   K. To perform daily religious and philosophical meditation
   L. To abstain from making a living by any of these means: agriculture, trade, military, crafts, singing and music.

KRISHNA CONSCIOUSNESS

Hare Krishnas are the ridiculed and often misunderstood followers of A.C. Bhaktivedanta Swami Prabhupada, the spiritual master of the Krishna Consciousness Movement, who came to the United States in 1965. This Hindu philosophy, based on the doctrine of Ahimsa and the *Bhagavad-gita*, has been growing steadily and setting up centers in the Western world. Hare Krishna followers do not eat meat or wear leather products. As a matter of fact, vegetarianism is essential to Krishna Consciousness, a philosophy demanding that a man must live strictly in tune with the laws of the god Krishna in order to be peaceful and prosperous. All unnecessary violence must be avoided.

Food has further religious overtones since nourishment is offered to Krishna and is another way of bringing a disciple back to the Godhead, the spiritual goal after death. Hare Krishnas base their vegetarianism on the *Bhagavad-gita* (as they do their whole belief), where it is written that only four foods were offered to the god Krishna: a leaf, a flower, fruit and water. These are interpreted as vegetables, grains, fruits, milk or water.

Krishna Consciousness divides life into three modes: goodness, passion and ignorance. Foods of goodness, such as milk, increase the duration of life. Passionate foods are hot and spicy. Foods of ignorance include old and decayed food as well as meat.

There is little sex in the Hare Krishna movement; most are allowed to indulge only once a month. They believe they have higher passions (Krishna, for example) and believe in saving their energy.

Cleanliness is another important principle for these followers, since the body is the statement of their purity and spirituality. They shower every time they go to the bathroom or are allowed at least two showers a day.

The Krishna Consciousness movement believes very strongly in the caste system. It believes the caste system is the law of God and those in it yearn to reach the level of Brahmin. The goal is eternal reunion with Krishna in a spiritual corner of the universe known to them as Viakunta.

Part Four
The Wisdom of Oriental Philosophy

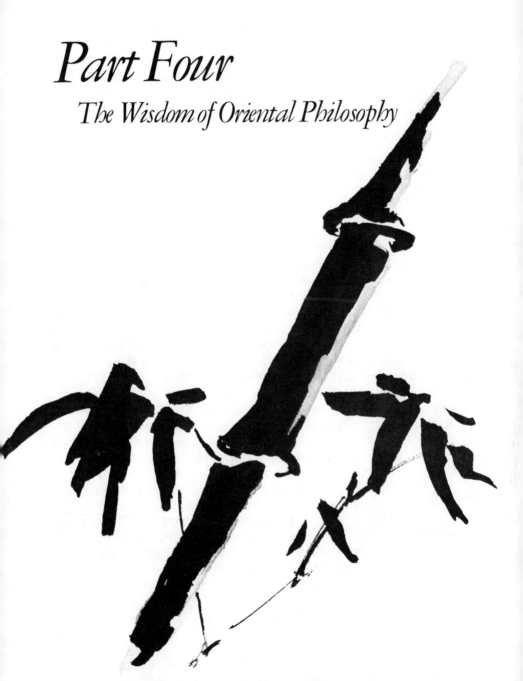

"To know is to know that to know is not to know."
—CONFUCIUS

CHAPTER NINE

"Wisdom of the Orient"

In this age of scientism and materialism, people throughout the world are plagued by unrest and self-alienation. Daily they stray from themselves, living for nothing but ephemeral pleasures. The Oriental Philosopher is the opposite of those people; he abides serenely in here and now, and is above joy and grief, life and death. It is not that he is without worries and afflictions, but seeing them with an awakened sense, he is enslaved by none of them. He is a man of complete freedom.

The literature of Oriental Philosophy is a treasurehouse of wisdom and inspiration. Oriental philosophical literature expresses the inexpressible. Outsiders will find something mystical about the inexpressible in whatever way it is represented, because of their lack of understanding of the topic. There is nothing mystical about any of the tidbits of knowledge presented. It may appear as such only because each of the selections of Oriental literature has both an outer and an inner meaning. From within they hold the key for enlightenment; they express a thought that will plunge the philosopher into the realm of satori. On the outside, they are an anecdote of truth, expressed in its highest form. Therefore, we can see that the writings are for a wide audience, the light reader and the deep, reflective meditator.

The following are poems, prayers, sermons and anecdotes of Hindu, Buddhist, Zen, Yogic, Taoist and Confucian literature, selected from the major texts of each of these philosophies. Each is an aid for meditation.

To begin meditation, you must first select a common place where you will perform this philosophizing. It must be quiet and spacious, devoid of any disturbing objects, and it should be well-ventilated. If you are in the country, an outdoor area is ideal;

at home, always choose the same place because it will develop a meditative atmosphere.

When beginning the meditation, you must try to rid your mind of any outside interference and disturbing thoughts and concentrate solely on the particular meditative aid you have chosen. At first you will find this impossible because each time you will try, your mind will wander into a multitude of worldly thoughts. Do not get frustrated during your first attempts at meditating. Each time you sense your being wandering from the wisdom of meditation, note where your thoughts are going and return to the state of reflection. To start off you must perform various breathing exercises.

Adopt any meditative pose (see Appendix One). Place the index finger of the right hand between the eyebrows, and close the left nostril with the second finger. Breathe in slowly and deeply through the right nostril, and when a full breath has been taken, close the right nostril, open the left nostril and breathe out through the left nostril. Now breathe in through the left nostril, close it, open the right nostril and exhale through it, then take a full breath using both nostrils together as in normal breathing. Repeat several times and then perform Rhythmic Breathing.

Rhythmic Breathing is performed the same as the above except this time the breathing is in tempo. Time the intake of air with the heart's beating. When inhaling with the right nostril count to four, in conjunction with four heartbeats. Now hold both nostrils closed and await the four beats, then exhale on the count of four. Thus the tempo is four-four-four. Perform this exercise for ten counts (that is, left and right cycles being one) and inhale with both left and right nostrils for a count of eight, hold four, exhale eight. Now the body is ready for reflective meditation.

Now the body is relaxed, there is no noise, and you have selected your meditative aid (some piece of wisdom). At this point, read it and reflect on its meaning. While in reflection, the breathing should be a natural six inhale, six hold, six exhale (six-six-six).

Read the meditative aid, repeat it several times. Close your eyes and meditate upon the meaning of the words. Start off with only a few minutes of meditation until you can concentrate several hours in such a practice.

The benefits? Several! A calm personality, wisdom when needed, never at a loss in a situation, healthier breathing habits and knowledge, the key to existence.

NOTE: All poems marked with an asterisk are by the author under his ordination name, Yama Roshi.)

1

I will now explain to you the yoga of mediation.

The first step to this yoga is observance of the moral precepts, which must be obeyed by all. These are:

Do your duties faithfully, no matter how lowly your conditions in life. Surrender the fruits of your actions to God. Seek the society of the holy and do service to them. Above all, acquire an eager thirst for righteousness, truth and freedom.

Practice meditation.

Practice moderation in your appetites. Do injury to no creature. Swerve not from the truth. Covet not the wealth of another.

Accept only enough for your daily needs.

Practice self-control and self-denial, that you may lead a pure, continent life. Before all else, be clean and pure in soul, mind and body.

And finally, study the Scriptures with diligence.

To practice meditation, one should select a secluded place and use it for that purpose only. When one is seated, he must practice control of prana (breath), with the help of breathing exercises. The mind must then be gathered in to itself and not permitted to dwell on external objects.

Next, the mind must be on one of the centers of consciousness within the body. This final act is known as the practice of concentration.

Thus prepared, one should meditate on the divine attributes.

Through these practices will come remarkable spiritual growth. By the practice of pranayama, you may acquire physical health.

As you practice pratyahara you may acquire physical withdrawal and a cessation of external objects. Practice of concentration will bring you purity of heart, and meditation will enable you to unite yourself with the divine.

Thus, when your mind and heart become calm and pure, you will learn to dwell in the consciousness of God. Then you will find divine love.

—From the *Srimad Bhagavatam*

2

Sozan, a Chinese Zen master, was asked by a student: "What is the most valuable thing in the world?"

The master replied: "The head of a dead cat."

"Why is the head of a dead cat the most valuable thing in the world?" inquired the student.

Sozan replied: "Because no one can name its price."

3

After Bankei had passed away, a blind man who lived near the master's temple told a friend: "Since I am blind, I cannot watch a person's face, so I must judge his character by the sound of his voice. Ordinarily when I hear someone congratulate another upon his happiness or success, I also hear a secret tone of envy. When condolence is expressed for the misfortune of another, I hear pleasure and satisfaction, as if the one condoling were really glad there was something left to gain in his own world.

"In all my experience, however, Bankei's voice was always sincere. Whenever he expressed sorrow, sorrow was all I heard. Whenever he expressed happiness, I heard nothing but happiness."

4

Calm, activity—each has its use. At times
This worldly dust piles mountain-high.
Now the neighbors sleep, I chant a sutra.
The incense burnt away, I sing before the moon.

Master Joshu and the dog—
Truly exorbitant, their foolishness.
Being and non-being at last
Annihilated, speak the final word!

> Soen
> Zen Master, Rinzai Sect
> 1859—1919

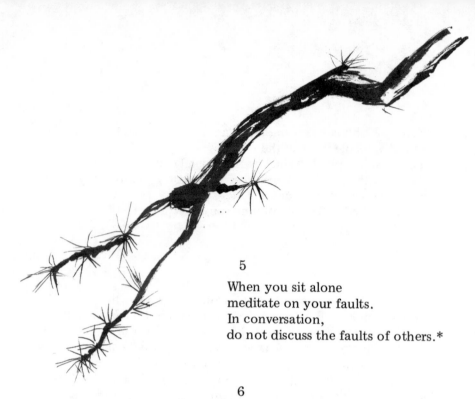

5

When you sit alone
meditate on your faults.
In conversation,
do not discuss the faults of others.*

6

Know what causes the bondage of the soul, and knowing, try to remove it.

All things are eternal by their very nature.

As imprisoned birds do not get out of their cage, so those ignorant of right or wrong do not get out of their misery.

There are three ways of committing sin: by our actions; by authorization of others and by approval.

A sage leads a life as far removed from love as from hate.

All living beings hate pain; therefore do not injure them or kill them. This is the essence of wisdom, not to kill anything.

Leave off pride, anger, deceit and greed.

Men suffer individually for the deeds they themselves have done.

The wise man should consider not that he alone suffers; all creatures in the world suffer.

Conceit is a very thin thorn; it is difficult to pull out.

No man should seek fame and respect for his austerities.

He who is purified by meditation is like a ship in the water which avoids all danger until it reaches the shore.

Do not maintain that there is no such thing as good and evil but that there *is* good and evil. —From the *Prakrit*
Translated by Hermann Jacobi

7

He who stands on his tiptoes does not stand firm;
He who stretches his legs does not walk easily.
So, he who displays himself does not shine;
He who asserts his own views is not distinguished;
He who exalts himself does not find merit acknowledged;
He who is self-conceited has no superiority allowed to him.

Such conditions, viewed from the standpoint of the Tao, are like remnants of food or a tumor on the body, which all dislike.

Hence those who pursue the course of the Tao do not adopt and allow them.

—Tao-Te-Ching

8

The pupils of Tendai Buddhism practiced meditation until Zen Buddhism entered their fine country. Four students who were intimate friends promised one another to observe seven days of silence.

On the first day all were silent. Their meditation had begun auspiciously, but when night came and the oil lamps were growing dim, one of the pupils could not help exclaiming to the servant:

"Fix those lamps."

The second pupil was surprised to hear the first one talk. "We are not supposed to say a word," he remarked.

"You two surprise me. You are stupid. Why did you talk?" asked the third.

"I am the only one who has not talked," concluded the fourth pupil.

9

This is what is meant by "achieving true knowledge:"

Confucius said: "In presiding over lawsuits, I am as good as anyone. The thing is, we should make it our aim that there may be no lawsuits at all, so that people who have actually done wrong will be too ashamed of themselves to indulge in words of self defense. Thus the people are inspired with a great respect or fear (of the magistrate). This is called 'to know the root (or bottom) of things.' This is called 'achieving true knowledge (or wisdom).' "

10

Open,
Our hearts change,
Like the endless cycles
Of autumn breeze.*

11

Confucius said: "The man who loves truth (or learning) is better than the man who knows it, and the man who finds happiness in it is better than the man who loves it."

12

The soul which is not moved, which takes sorrow and joy indifferently, lives in the life undying.

* * *

Birthless and deathless and changeless remains the spirit, dead though the house of it seems.

* * *

Find the reward in doing right, in right.

* * *

Scorn those who follow virtue for her gifts.

* * *

Because they seek no gain, the right-hearted rise more certainly from the bonds of body, step-by-step, to the highest bliss.

* * *

The mind that follows the senses sees its helm of wisdom torn away, and, like a ship in a storm, drives to wreck and death.

* * *

The world is strong, but what discerns it is stronger, and the mind strongest; and high over all the ruling soul.

—From the *Bhagavad-gita*

13

"Our schoolmaster used to take a nap every afternoon," related a student of Zen Master Soyen Shaku. "We children asked him why he did it and he told us:

" 'I go to dreamland to meet the old sages just as Confucius did.'

"When Confucius slept, he would dream of ancient sages and later tell his followers about them.

"It was extremely hot one day so some of us took a nap. Our schoolmaster scolded us. 'We went to dreamland to meet the ancient sages the same as Confucius did,' we explained. 'What were the messages from those sages?' our schoolmaster demanded. One of us replied: 'We went to dreamland and met the sages and asked them if our schoolmaster came there every afternoon, but they said they had never seen such a fellow.' "

14

Who knows no limitation
will have cause to lament.*

15

"To what extent is the world called 'empty,' Lord?"

"Because it is empty of self or what belongs to self, it is therefore said: 'The world is empty.' And what is empty of self and what belongs to self? The eye, material shapes, visual consciousness, impression on the eye—all these are empty of self and of what belongs to self. So too are ear, nose, tongue, body and mind (and their appropriate sense-data, appropriate consciousness and the impression on them of their appropriate sense-data—as above), all empty of self and of what belongs to self. Also, that feeling which arises, conditioned by impression on the eye, ear, nose, tongue, body, mind, whether it be pleasant or painful or neither painful nor pleasant—that too is empty of self and of what belongs to self. Wherefore is the world called empty because it is empty of self and of what belongs to self."

—*Samyutta-nikaya Sutra*

16

Fishing baskets are employed to catch fish; but when the fish are got, the men forget the baskets. Snares are employed to catch hares; but when the hares are got, men forget the snares. Words are employed to convey ideas; but when the ideas are truly comprehended, men forget the words. Fain would I talk to someone who has forgotten the words.

—Chuang-tse

17

He who has reached the stage of thought is silent.
He who has attained perfect knowledge is also silent.
He who uses silence in lieu of speech really does speak.
He, who for knowledge substitutes blankness of mind, really does know. Without words and speaking not, without knowledge and knowing not, he really speaks and really knows.
Saying nothing and knowing nothing, there is in reality nothing that he does not say, nothing that he does not know. This is how the matter stands; there is nothing more to be said.

—Lieh-tse

18

Yao, the wise man, was looking around at Hwa when he was approached by the border-warden who said, "Ha! the sage! Let me ask blessings on the sage! May he live long!"

Yao said, "Hush!" But the other went on, "May the sage become rich!"

Yao said again, "Hush!"

But the warden continued, "May the sage have many sons!"

When Yao repeated his "Hush!", the warden said, "Long life, riches, and many sons are what men wish for . . . . How is it that you alone do not wish for them?"

Yao replied, "Many sons bring many fears; riches bring many troubles; and long life gives rise to slander."

—Chuang-tse

19

In Tokyo in the Meiji Period there lived two great Zen masters of opposite sects and characteristics. One, Unsho, an instructor in Shingon Buddhism, kept Buddha's precepts scrupulously. He never drank intoxicants, nor did he eat after eleven o'clock in the morning. The other teacher, Tanzan, a master of philosophy, never observed the precepts. When he felt like eating he ate, and when he felt like sleeping in the daytime he slept.

One day Unsho visited Tanzan, who was drinking wine at the time, not even a drop of which was supposed to touch the tongue of the Buddhist.

"Hello, brother," Tanzan greeted him. "Won't you join me in a friendly drink?"

"I never drink!" exclaimed Unsho solemnly.

"One who does not drink is not even human," said Tanzan.

"Do you mean to call me inhuman just because I do not indulge in intoxicating liquids!" exclaimed Unsho in anger. "Then if I am not human, what am I?"

"A Buddha," answered Tanzan.

20

The way to which mankind may hold
Is not the eternal way.
Eternal truths cannot be told

In what men write or say.
The name that may be named by man
  Is not the eternal name
That was before the world began
  Or human language came.
In that nameable took root
  The tree of fire and force,
Which, having blossomed and borne fruit,
  Returns then to its source.
Who warms his body at that fire,
  Sees nothing but its smoke;
But he who puts aside desire,
  The flame's self may invoke.

—*Tao-Te-Ching*

21

The king said: "Bhanto Nagasena, does rebirth take place without anything transmigrating (passing over)?"

"Yes, Your Majesty. Rebirth takes place without anything transmigrating."

"How, Bhanto Nagasena, does rebirth take place without anything transmigrating? Give an example."

"Suppose, Your Majesty, a man were to light a light from another light; pray, would the one light have passed over (transmigrated) to the other light?"

"No, verily, Bhanto."

"In exactly the same way, Your Majesty, does rebirth take place without anything transmigrating."

"Give another example."

"Do you remember, Your Majesty, having learned, when you were a boy, some verse or other from your professor of poetry?"

"Yes, Bhanto."

"Pray, Your Majesty, did the verse pass over (transmigrate) from your teacher to you?"

"No, verily, Bhanto."

"In exactly the same way, Your Majesty, does rebirth take place without anything transmigrating."

"Bhanto Nagasena," said the king, "what is it that is born into the next existence?"

"Your Majesty," said the elder, "it is name and form that are born into the next existence."

22

Open the door

look!

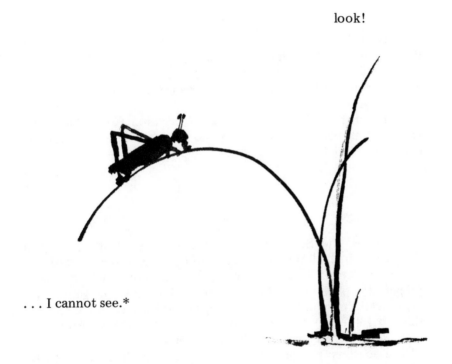

. . . I cannot see.*

23

"To wear out one's intellect in an obstinate adherence to the individuality of things, not recognizing the fact that all things are ONE—this is called 'three in the morning.' "

Chuang-tse, who made the comment, explained his meaning of the phrase "three in the morning" in the following story:

"A keeper of monkeys said with regard to their ration of chestnuts that each monkey was to have three in the morning and four at night. But at this the monkeys were very angry, so the keeper said they might have four in the morning and three at night, with which arrangement they were all well pleased. The actual number of chestnuts remained the same, but there was an adaptation to the likes and dislikes of those concerned. Such is the principle of putting oneself into subjective relation with externals."

24

It is said that the Superior Man has two things in which he delights, and to be ruler over the empire is not one of them.

That the father and mother are both alive and that the condition of his brothers affords no cause for anxiety, this is one delight.

That when looking up he has no occasion for shame before Heaven, and below he has no occasion to blush before men, this is his second delight.

—Mencius

25

As usual, the Soto Zen master Fugai was planning his great dinner to which all the Zen masters of every sect were invited.

Circumstances arose on the day of the dinner which delayed preparation of the food. In haste the cook went to the garden with his curved knife and cut off the tops of green vegetables, chopped them together, and made soup, unaware that in his haste he had included a part of a snake in the vegetables.

The masters thought they never tasted such good soup. But when Fugai himself found the snake's head in his bowl, he summoned the cook.

"What is this?" questioned Fugai, holding up the head of the snake.

"Oh, thank you, master," replied the cook, taking the morsel and eating it quickly.

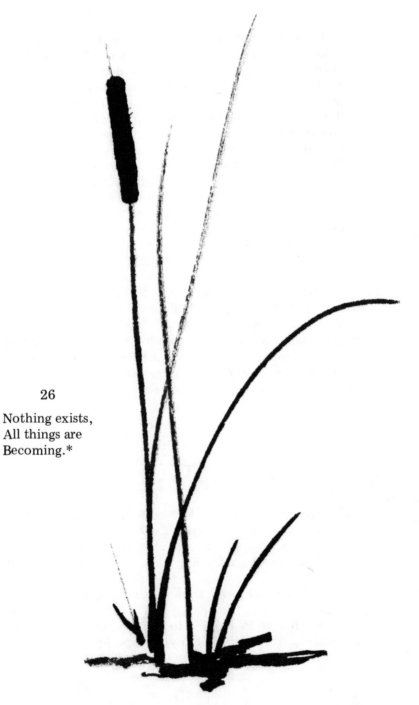

26

Nothing exists,
All things are
Becoming.*

27

In the heart of all things, of whatever is in the universe, dwells the Lord. He alone is the reality. Wherefore, renouncing vain appearances, rejoice in him. Covet no man's wealth.

Well may he be content to live a hundred years who acts without attachment—who works his work with earnestness, but without desire, not yearning for its fruits—he and he alone.

Worlds there are without suns, covered up with darkness. To these after death go the ignorant, slayers of the Self.

The Self is One. Unmoving sun, it moves swifter than thought. The senses do not overtake it, for always it goes before. Remaining still, it outstrips all that run. Without the Self, there is no life.

To the ignorant, the Self appears to move—yet it moves not. From the ignorant it is far distant—yet it is near. It is within all, and it is without all.

He who sees all beings in the Self, and the Self in all beings, hates none.

To the illuminated soul, the Self is all. For him who sees everywhere oneness, how can there be grief and delusion?

The Self is everywhere. Bright is he, bodiless, without scar or imperfection, without bone, without flesh, pure, untouched by evil. The Seer, the Thinker, the One who is above all, the Self-Existent—he it is that has established perfect order among objects and beings from beginningless time.

—The *Upanishads*

28

The Kegon master Jinjo refused to teach, but from time to time would advise people about the way to proceed on the Path.

One day a disciple, who was incapable of learning and regularly driven abnormal by attending "mystical ceremonies," visited him. He asked:

"How can I best profit from the teachings of the sages?"

Jinjo said:

"I am happy to be able to tell you that I have an infallible method which corresponds to your capacity."

"And what, pray, Kegon Jinjo, is that?"

"Simply stop up your ears and think about radishes."
"Before, during or after the lectures and exercises?"
"Instead of attending any of them."

29

There is a story told by word of mouth about the conversation that took place between Bodhidharma and his master Prajnatara before leaving India to go to China.

* * *

Bodhidharma questioned his master:

"Tell me, what is the most appreciated gift of man? It is necessary when going to kings to bear precious gifts; only vile men approach them with empty hands."

Prajnatara replied:

"If you follow my advice, you will take to the country what is not found there. Is it fitting that one should take what is there already? True knowledge is found there, secrets are found there, obedience to higher beings is found there. Take then the ardor of love and the longing of the spirit; no one can offer other than this. If a single sigh of love goes to that place it will carry the perfume of the heart. That place is consecrated to the essence of the soul. If a man should heave one sigh of true contrition he will forthwith be in possession of salvation."

30

The benefit of reading varies directly with one's experience in life. It is like looking at the moon.

A young reader may be compared to one seeing the moon through a single crack, a middle-aged reader seems to see it from an enclosed courtyard, and an old man seems to see it from an open terrace, with a complete view of the entire field.

—Chang Chao

31

Thus it is that there are few men in the world who love and at the same time know the bad qualities of the object of their love, or who hate and yet know the excellences of the object of their hatred.

—From the *Ta Hsueh* (*Great Learning*)

32

Zuigan called out to himself every day: "Master."
Then he answered himself: "Yes, sir."
And after that he added: "Become sober."
Again he answered: "Yes, sir."
"And after that," he continued, "do not be deceived by others."
"Yes, sir; yes, sir," he answered.

—From the *Mumonkan*

33

There is no other door to
   knowledge than the door love opens;
And there is no truth
   except the truth we discover
In love.*

34

The Zen master Bankei's talks were not only attended by masters and students of every religious and philosophical sect, but also high-ranking government officials. He never quoted Scriptures, nor talked in philosophical riddles or scholastic dissertations. Instead, he talked from deep within his heart and touched the heart of all his listeners.

His large audiences angered a priest of the Nichiren sect because the adherents had left to hear about Zen. The proud Nichiren priest came to the sermon, determined to undermine Bankei.

"Hey, Zen master!" he shouted within the crowd. "Hold on a second. Whoever respects you will obey what you say, but a man like me does not respect you. Can you make me obey you?"

"Come up beside me and I will show you," said Bankei.

The self-centered priest pushed his way through the followers to the teacher.

Bankei smiled. "Come over to my left side."

The priest obeyed.

"No, no!" said Bankei, "We could talk much better if you were on my right side. My right ear can hear much better."

The priest proudly stepped over to the right.

"You see," said Bankei, "you are obeying me and I think you are a very gentle fellow. Now sit down and listen."

35

The Samurai were a warrior sect in Japan up until 1873. Their way of fighting was not only very effective, being a mixture of fencing (ken-jutsu) and unarmed combat (jujutsu), but it was also considered a way of life. The Samurai followed a code of ethics called "bushido" and also diligently studied Zen for a two-fold reason. It helped to look at life and death indifferently, making it possible for the soldier to fight better, and it gave him peace of mind.

* * *

A Samurai named Nobushige came to Zen master Hakuin, and asked him: "Is there really a heaven (paradise) and a hell?"

"Who are you?" inquired the Zen master.

"I am a soldier. I follow bushido and wish to know the secrets of life hereafter."

"You, a Samurai!" exclaimed Hakuin. "What king would want you as his guard. Your face looks like that of a beggar."

Nobushige became so angered that he began to draw his sword, but Hakuin continued: "So you play with a sword. Your blade is probably so dull that it could not even cut off the head of a priest."

As Nobushige drew his sword Hakuin remarked: "Here opens the gates of hell."

At those words the Samurai, perceiving the master's lesson, sheathed his sword and bowed.

"Here opens the gates of paradise (heaven)," said Hakuin.

36

Some madman shrieks on the mountain top, and upon hearing the echo far below, may go to seek it in the valley. Once in the valley, he shrieks again and straightway climbs to search back among the peaks. Such a man may spend a thousand rebirths searching for the source of these sounds by following their echoes. Far better that you make no sound, for then there will be no echo and you will be one with the dwellers of Nirvana.

—Huang Po
Founder
Obato Zen Sect

37

There is nothing more visible than what is secret, and nothing more manifest than what is minute; therefore, the Superior Man is watchful over himself even when alone.

—From the *Chung Yung*

38

Jinjo once disappeared from Japan, no one knew where. At last he was discovered in the house of the ill, sitting with humid eye and dry lips among these grotesque creatures.

His friend said: "This is no place for you who are a master of divine mysteries."

Jinjo replied: "These persons, in the way of religion, are neither men nor women. I am as they. I sink in inertia, as my virility is a reproach. If you use praise and blame to make distinctions you are creating idols. When you conceal a hundred idols under your kimono, why appear before men as a master?"

39

Chang Tsze asked how a man might conduct himself so as to be appreciated everywhere. Confucius said:

"Let his words be sincere and truthful and his actions honorable and careful. Such conduct may be practiced among the rude tribes of the South and North. If his words be not sincere and truthful and his actions not honorable and careful, will he with such conduct be appreciated even in his own neighborhood?"

40

Love is the shadow of
     the evening,
Which strengthens with the
     setting sun of life.*

41

The Buddha said:

"You should ponder on the fact that, though each of the four elements of which the body is made up has a name, they none of them (constitute any part of) the real self. In fact, the self is nonexistent, like a mirage."

—From the *Sutra of Forty-two Sections*

42

MASTER: Where is there evil? In the rat whose nature it is to steal grain or in the cat, whose nature it is to kill the rat?

STUDENT: The rat steals and is thus evil, and the cat sees him in his evil and punishes.

MASTER: And to the rat, the cat is evil, stopping him from doing his own nature.

STUDENT: Yet, master, one must surely be evil.

MASTER: The rat does not steal, the cat does not kill. Rain falls, the river flows, the mountain remains. Each acts according to the nature God has given it. Not to act according to your nature is to throw the wheel of becoming off its axle.

STUDENT: Then there is no evil in our fellow men? Each man sees what he does as being good and in his *way.*

MASTER: Friend, a man may tell himself many things, but is the universe and all of creation made up of just that single, absolute man?

STUDENT: If a man does harm to me, I will return harm; it will teach him never to injure another man. Thus, we will have complete harmony.

MASTER: And what if you did nothing at all. What then?

STUDENT: He will go on all the days of his life believing he can do harm to others.

MASTER: Perhaps. Or perhaps he will learn that some people are injured and in their pain return only kindness.

43

Honor and riches, distinctions and austerity, fame and profit, these six things produce the impulses of the will.

Personal appearance and deportment, the desire of beauty and subtle reasoning, excitement of the breath and cherishing thoughts, these six things produce the errors of the mind.

Hatred and longings, joy and anger, grief and delight, these things are the entanglements of virtue.

Refusal and reproachments, receiving and giving, knowledge and ability, these six things obstruct the way of the sagely-minded man.

When these four conditions, with their six causes each, do not agitate the breast, the mind is correct. Being correct, it is still; being still, it is pellucid; being pellucid, it is free from preoccupation; being free from preoccupation, it is in a state of inaction, in which it accomplishes everything.

—Chuang-tse

44

Kitagaki, the governor of Kyoto, called upon the great Zen master of Tofukuji Temple, Master Keichu. He gave the attendant monk his calling card to present to Keichu. The card read: "Kitagaki, Governor of Kyoto." Keichu looked at the card and said, "I have no business with such a fellow. Tell him to get out of here!" The attendant carried the calling card back with an apology.

"No, that was my error," the governor said. He took the card, scratched out the words "Governor of Kyoto," and said, "Please take this back and ask your master again."

When Keichu saw the card he said, "Oh, is that Kitagaki? I want to see that fellow."

45

Those who dream of the pleasure of drinking may in the morning wail and weep. Those who dream of wailing and weeping may in the morning be going out to hunt. When they were dreaming they did not know it was a dream; but when they awoke they knew it was a dream.

Thus it is said that there is the Great Awakening, after which we shall know that this life was a great dream, while all the while the stupid think that they are awake.

—Chuang-tse

46

Seek not to know the answers,
But to understand the questions.*

47

A Zen student came to Bankei and complained, "Master, I have an ungovernable temper. How can I cure it?"

"You have something that is very strange," said Bankei. "Let me see what you have."

"I cannot show you just now," said the student.

"When can you show me?" asked Bankei.

"It arises unexpectedly," replied the other.

"Then it must not be your own true nature. If it were, you could show it to me at any time. It is something you are not born with. It is not you."

48

A Zen master living as a hermit on a mountain was asked by a monk, "What is the Way?"

"What a fine mountain this is," the master replied.

"I am not asking about the mountain. I am asking about the Way."

"So long as you cannot go beyond the mountain, my son, you cannot reach the Way."

49

Some children were playing beside the river's bed. They made sand castles, and each defended his castle by saying, "This castle is mine only." They kept their castles separate and would not allow any mistake of ownership. When the castles were completed, one child kicked over someone else's castle and completely destroyed it. The child who built the structure broke into rage, pulled the other child's hair, struck him with his fist and beat him. He then called out, "He has spoiled my castle! Come along all of you and help me to punish him as he deserves." The others all came to his help. They beat the child with sticks and then stamped on him as he lay flat on the ground.

When they had finished their punishment, they went back to their sand castles, each saying, "This is mine; no one else may play with it. Keep away, don't touch my castle!"

As evening came, it was getting too dark to play and they all thought to go home. No one now cared what became of his castle. One child stamped on his, another pushed it over with his hands, allowing the sand to filter through his fingers. They turned away and went back, each to his home.

—*Yogacara Bhumi Sutra*

50

OM . . .†

Filled with Brahman are the things we see,
Filled with Brahman are the things we do not see,
From out of Brahman all—yet it is still the same,

Lead me from the unreal to the real.
Lead me from darkness to light.
Lead me from death to immortality.

—From the *Brihadaranyaka Upanishad*

51

The Ts'ao-T'ung (Soto) Zen sect, during meditation, applies the following five principles:

1. It is sufficient to sit in meditation, without having a subject of meditation.

2. Sitting in meditation and Awakening are not two different things.

3. One must not wait for Awakening.

4. There is no Awakening to obtain.

5. Mind and body must become one.

†The greatest mantra or word of power. When properly recited by a suitable person, this word—which is the indicator of divine power—produces great harmony in the body and in the mind. The mental effects are greater when it is uttered only mentally, but in any case it should not be very loud, and it should be uttered in a floating way, as it were, not with force.

It is made up of three letters—A, U and M. The two vowels A and U blend into the O. M is sounded without parting the lips, so the whole word sounds like "home" without the H, but somewhat prolonged according to the desire and intuition of the person reciting. The theory of Om is that as A is the first sound, made at the back of the mouth, and M is the last, made with the lips, and the U is in the nature of a glide between them, the word covers the whole range of vowels, which are the power in speech. Consonants represent only the limitations or applications of this power. This whole word is the expression of creation, indicating the presence of the Creator.

Indeed, the whole range of creation is indicated, as the A, U and M are respectively associated with the divine powers or functions symbolized by three devas or gods: Brahman, Vishnu and Shiva.

Om is recited by Hindus at the beginning of prayers, hymns and words of worship or aspiration. It is also used at the end, or with the addition of "Shanti" (peace) repeated three times.

52

Koan

The Great Master Bodhidharma goes to the Sil-lum temple at Honan. For nine years he sits facing the wall.

Commentary

Watch out, don't go on sleeping!

Poem

The giant bird has taken a lot of trouble
To reach the southern sea,
But he regrets the long, long distance traversed.
Last night, we drank too much at the Great Festival;
This morning, it's more difficult to awaken.

53

"Reverend Nagasena, what is the herb-shop of the Enlightened One, the Buddha?"

There are herbs, great king, proclaimed by the Enlightened One, with which herbs the Buddha cures both gods and men, to wit: meditations, the Three Signs of Being, the right exertions, the Seven Principles of Form, the Four Noble Truths, the Noble Eightfold Path. With these herbs the Buddha purges Wrong Views, purges Wrong Resolution, purges Wrong Speech, purges Wrong Conduct, purges Wrong Means of Livelihood, purges Wrong Exertion, purges Wrong Mindfulness, purges Wrong Concentration; produces vomiting of Desire, produces vomiting of Ill Will, produces vomiting of Delusion, produces vomiting of Pride, produces vomiting of Flash Views, produces vomiting of Doubt, produces vomiting of Arrogance, produces vomiting of Sloth and Torpor, produces vomiting of Shamelessness or Fearlessness of Wrongdoing.

This, great king, is what is meant by the herb-shop of the Enlightened One.

—From the *Questions of King Milinda*

54

Sir, why is the world called empty?

It is because in the world identities and things possessing this identity do not exist.

What are the things which do not have identity?

Eye, image and sight do not possess identity nor that which belongs to identity. In the same way, ear, nose, tongue, body, thoughts, their object and their knowledge, do not possess identity either, nor that which belongs to identity.

—*Samyutta Nikaya Sutra*

55

Nirvana is like . . .

It is like a plantation tree which is hollow inside.

It is like a phantom caused by a conjurer.

It is like a dream giving false ideas.

It is like the moon producing a shadow.

It is like an echo produced by various relations.

It is like a floating cloud that changes and vanishes.

It is like lightning which instantly comes and goes.

It has no duality as the fire has none.

It is empty when freed from false ideas of me and mine.

—*Vimalakirti Sutra*

56

The fishes, though deep in the water, may be hooked; the birds, though high in the air, may be shot. But man's secret thoughts are out of reach.

The heavens may be measured, the earth may be surveyed, but the heart of man is not to be known.*

57

When Bankei was walking through a market, he overheard a conversation between a butcher and his customer.

"Give me the best piece of meat you have," said the customer.

"Everything in my shop is the best," replied the butcher. "You cannot find here any piece of meat that is not best."

At these words Bankei reached satori.

58

Past, present, future: unattainable,
Yet clear as the moteless sky.
Late at night, the stool's cold as iron,
But the moonlit window smells of plum.

Priceless is one's incantation,
Turning a red-hot iron ball to butter oil.
Heaven? Purgatory? Hell?
Snowflakes fallen on the hearth fire.

How lacking in permanence the minds of the sentient—
They are the consummate Nirvana of all BUDDHAS.
A wooden hen, egg in mouth, straddles the coffin.
An earthenware horse breaks like wind for satori-land.

You no sooner attain the great void
Than the body and mind are lost together.
Heaven and hell—a straw.
The Buddha-realm, Pandemonium—shambles.
Listen: a nightingale strains her voice, serenading the snow.
Look: a tortoise wearing a sword climbs the lampstand.
Should you desire the great tranquility,
Prepare to sweat white beads.

—Hakuin
Rinzai Zen Master
1685–1768

59

Mokusen Hiki was living in a temple in the province of Tampa.
One of his students complained of the strictness of his wife.

Mokusen visited the woman and showed her his clenched fist
before her face.

"What do you mean by that?" asked the surprised woman.

"Suppose my fist were always like that. What would you call
it?" he asked.

"Deformed," replied the woman.

Then he opened his hand flat in her face and asked: "Suppose it were always like this. What then?"

"Another kind of deformity," said the wife.

"If you understand that much," finished Mokusen, "you are a good wife." Then he left.

After his visit, this wife helped her husband to distribute as well as to save.

60

Before a man studies the Philosophies of the Orient, to him mountains are mountains and waters are waters; after he gets insight into the truth of Philosophy through the instruction of a good master, mountains to him are no longer mountains and waters are not waters. But after this, when he really attains to the abode of rest, mountains are once again mountains and waters are waters.

61

"Bring me," he said to his son, "a fruit from a banyan tree."

"Here is one, sir."

"Break it."

"It is broken, master."

"What do you see there?"

"Some seeds, exceeding small."

"Break one of these."

"It is broken, master."

"What do you see there?"

"Nothing at all."

The father told his son: "My son, that subtle essence which you do not see there—in that essence stands the being of the great banyan tree. In that which is the subtle self, all that exists has its essence. That is the True, that is the Self."

"Pray, master," said the son, "tell me more."

For the second lesson the father gave his son a bag of salt, saying, "Place this salt in a vessel of water and come to me tomorrow morning as usual."

When the son appeared the next day the father commanded, "Bring me the salt which you put in the water."

But the salt had disappeared.

"Taste the water from the top of the vessel and tell me how it is."

"Salty," said the son.

"And from the middle?"

"Salty."

"And from the bottom."

"Salty, also."

The father said: "Here likewise in this body of yours, my son, you do not perceive the True; but there in fact it is. In that which is the subtle essence, all that exists has its Self."

—From the *Chandogya Upanishad*

62

The attempt, with what is not even, to produce what is even will only produce an uneven result.

The attempt, with what is uncertain, to make the certain will leave the uncertainty as it was.

He who uses only the sight of his eye is acted on by what he sees; it is the intuition of the spirit that gives the assurance of certainty.

That the sight of the eyes is not equal to the intuition of the spirit is a thing long acknowledged. And yet stupid people rely on what they see—is it not sad?

—Chuang-tse

63

The Superior Man prizes three things. The first is gentleness, the second is frugality, the third is humility. By being gentle he can be bold; by being frugal, he can be liberal, and by being humble he becomes a leader among men.

—Lao-tse

64

Spring rain;
How calmly
It falls.*

65

Among the greatest treasures to be found
    on earth,
Being of Nothingness is the greatest.*

66

Tanzan and Ekido were once traveling together down a muddy road. A heavy rain began falling, drenching both the masters.

Coming down the bend, they met a lovely girl in a silk kimono and sash, unable to cross the intersection.

"Come on, woman," said Tanzan at once. Lifting her in his arms, he carried her over the mud.

Ekido did not speak again until that night when they reached a lodging temple. Then he no longer could hold back his questions. "We monks don't go near females," he told Tanzan, "especially young and lovely ones. It is dangerous. Why did you do it?"

"I left the girl there," said Tanzan. "Are you still carrying her?"

67

Koan

A philosopher asked Buddha, whom he came to consult, to neither speak nor be silent.

Commentary

Other than my own family,
Who would dare to talk with their eyes blindfolded?

Verse

> It is known that it is difficult,
> Difficult to shut once more
> The door of the prison?
> Words and speech disappear,
> No support remains;
> If it is not a good horse,
> How can it succeed
> In such an admirable way?

68

Kaishu, a Rinzai Zen master (1808—1878), and his friends were crossing a turbulent river during a storm, and the boat pitched violently. All the master's friends were frightened and lost color, and some of them went as far as to call the goddess of love (Avalokitesvara) to their aid. But Kaishu sat quietly in zazen meditation.

When the boat made shore and his friends sighed with relief,

Kaishu reprimanded them with the following: "The Zenist is good for nothing if he can't help himself. The goddess must have laughed in your face."

69

Do not follow the evil law! Do not live on in thoughtlessness! Do not follow false doctrines! Be not a friend of the world!

Rouse thyself! Do not be idle! Follow the law of virtue! The virtuous rest in bliss in this world and in the next.

Follow the law of virtue; do not follow that of sin. The virtuous rest in bliss in this world and in the next.

—From the *Dhammapada*

70

They blossom and fall.
Their falling brings the sound
of morning
And last night's dream.*

71

Now concentration is explained.

Yoga is restraining of the mind-stuff (Chitta) from taking various forms (Virittis).

At that time (the time of concentration) the seer (Purusha) rests in his own modified state.

At other times (other than those of concentration) the seer is identified with the modifications.

There are five classes of modification, (some) painful and others not painful.

(These are) right knowledge, indiscrimination, verbal delusion, sleep and memory.

Direct perception, inference and competent evidence are proofs.

Indiscrimination is false knowledge not established in real nature.

Verbal delusion follows from words having no (corresponding) reality.

Sleep is Viritti which embraces the feeling of voidness.

Memory is when (Virittis of) perceived subjects do not slip away (and through impressions come back to consciousness).

—Patanjali, *Yoga Aphorisms*

72

King Hsuan of Ch'u asked his ministers, "I hear the people in the north are afraid of Chao Hsisu. Is this true?" The ministers did not make any reply, but Chiang Yi said to the King, "There was a tiger that was looking for animals for food and got hold of a fox. And the fox said, 'How dare you eat me? God in Heaven has made me chief of the animal kingdom. If you eat me you will be sinning against God. If you do not believe what I say, come along. I shall walk in front and you follow behind.' The tiger went along with the fox accordingly, and the animals fled at their approach. The tiger was not aware that the animals were not afraid of the fox, but of himself. Now, Your Royal Highness has a territory of five thousand square li and an army of a million soldiers, and you gave the entire power to Chao Hsisu. Therefore the people of the north are afraid of his power while they are really afraid of the King's army, as the animals were afraid of the tiger."

—Parable of the Tiger and the Fox, Chankuots'eh

73

The student Tokusan used to come to the master Ryutan in the evenings to talk and to listen. One night it was very late before he had finished asking questions.

"Why don't you go to bed?" asked Ryutan.

Tokusan bowed and lifted the screen to go out. "The hall is very dark," he said.

"Here, take this candle," said Ryutan, lighting one for the student.

Tokusan reached out his hand and took the candle.

Ryutan leaned forward and blew it out.

Appendixes

Chronology of Oriental Philosophical Literature

INDIA

Philosophical History	Literature (philosophy texts)
I. Vedic Age (1200—500 B.C.)	
1200 B.C. — Indo-Aryan society of Indus River Basin at first tribal, patriarchal and pastoral; later monarchical and agricultural.	Vedic literature is written and used to present philosophical concepts: 1) *Rig-veda* 2) *Yajur-veda* 3) *Sama-veda* 4) *Atharva-veda*
800 — Growth of Brahmin caste, ritual. Growth of mythology: deities, Indra, Varuna, Mitra, Soma.	800—600 — *Brahmanas*, books explaining the *Vedas*.
600 — Brahma, which was just a form of prayer, becomes associated with cosmic reality; Atman as a counterpart of Brahma. Doctrines of Karma, Samsara.	600—300 — *Upanishads* were written.
599—527 — Jainism (religion) founded by Vardhamana Mahavira.	
563—483 — Siddhartha Gotama founds Buddhism.	500 — Brahmi script in use.
II. Epic and Buddhist Age (500 B.C.—A.D.)	
Indian Trimurti (trinity): Brahma Vishnu Shiva New pessimistic spirit traceable to Buddhism. Doctrine of maya (illusion).	Period of composition of two great epics by slow accretion. Development of Sloka verse (four octosyllabic lines). *Mahabharata* (in 100,000 slokas) based on a 10th Century B.C. battle. Contains stories of Rama and Shakuntala as well as the *Bhagavad-gita*.
Main schools of Indian Philosophy: Sankhya — atheistic dualism Yoga — asceticism Mimamsa — Vedic doctrine of salvation by works Vedanta — Vedic doctrine of salvation by knowledge.	*Ramayana* (in 24,000 slokas) — epic poem attributed to Valmiki.
400 — Panini born; noted grammarian.	
327—325 — Alexander the Great—conquest of Punjab. Contact with Greece may have influenced Buddhist and Hindu Philosophy.	Simultaneous growth of: 1) Later Vedic literature (*Puranas*). 2) New Sanskrit literature. 3) Buddhist texts in Pali language.
274—236 — King Asoka established canons of Buddhism, helped spread Buddhism.	
150 — Patanjali. Writing of Yogic Scripture.	Buddhist *Tripitakas* (*Three Baskets*): 1) *Sutra* (doctrine) 2) *Vinaya* (monastic code) 3) *Abidharma* (philosophy)
	1st Century — *Dhammapada* (Buddhist Scripture) composed.

III. Classical Age (A.D.—1000 A.D.)

300 B.C. — Arthashastra, science and art of government.

200 B.C. to A.D. 200 — *The Laws of Manu*, philosophical and moral treatise.

4th Century A.D. — *Kamasutra* an influence on people (doctrine of reaching Nirvana by sex).

320—480 — Revival of Brahmanism by Chandragupta.

Spread of Indian Culture outside of India.

Prevalence of Vishnu, Shiva and Kali worship.

IV. Medieval and Modern Age (A.D. 1000—Present)

10th Century — Temple of Somnath sacked by Moslem rulers.

1194 — Afghan capture of Benares and destruction of the Center of Buddhist Philosophy.

1469 — Nanak, founder of Sikh Philosophy.

1582 — Akbar Padishad establishes a universal faith and philosophy based on all creeds.

1869—1948 — Mahatma Gandhi.

1947 — Indian Independence.

Sanskrit language flourishes.

Asvaghosa wrote down the life of Buddha.

CHINA

Philosophical History

I. First Millennium (c. 1100 B.C.—207 B.C.)

1. Chou Dynasties (c. 1100 B.C.—221 B.C.)

To c. 800 B.C. — Legendary age.

770—500 — Feudal Period, all states under Chou reign. Bamboo tablets used. Ancient documents collected; respect of history and love of music and poetry.

Philosophical speculation in schools of Confucianism, Lao-tse, Mo Ti and the Legalists.

Literature (philosophy texts)

479 — Confucius, edited five texts, authored the *Spring and Autumn Annals* and conversations in *Analects.*

6th Century — Lao-tse, semi-legendary founder of Taoism.

5th Century — Mo Ti, author of the *Mo-tse*, an anti-Confucian text.

4th Century — *Tao-Te-Ching*, chief book of Taoism; *Chuang-tse*, chief book of mystic Taoism.

332—296 — Mencius, Confucian scholar.

332—296 — Chu Yuan, author of the poem *Li Sao* (*"Falling into Trouble"*).

2. Ch'in Dynasty (221—207 B.C.)

Emperor Shih Huang (First Emperor), builder of the Great Wall.

Roll silk and camel's hair brush used in writing and brush drawing.

Scripture simplified and standardized.

213 — Nonscientific books burned and authors put to death.

II. Second Millennium (207 B.C.—960 A.D.)

1. Han Dynasties (207 B.C.—220 A.D.)

Capital at Loyang.

Restoration of learning and discovery of *Book of History.*

145 B.C. — Ssu Ma Ch'ien, father of Chinese History.

136 — *Five Classics* established: *Book of Changes, Odes, History, Annals* and *Rituals.*

1st and 2nd Centuries — Wars against the Huns. Buddhism introduced; Taoism as a cult of magic.

1st Century — Paper perfected.

220—264 — Empire divided into three kingdoms.

3rd Century — Lu Chi, criticism of scholarly texts.

2. Chin and Minor Dynasties (A.D. 265—618)

Capital at Nanking; little literature. Tea is used throughout China.

5th Century — Growth of Buddhism after Fa Hsien's journey to India. Buddhist cave-temples built.

365—427 — Tao Chien, major philosophical poet.

501—531 — Hsiao T'ung, published selected works of great philosophers.

606 A.D. — Master of Arts Degree examination instituted by Emperor Yang Ti.

3. T'ang and Five Dynasties (A.D. 618—960)

Period of high culture, especially in poetry. Pure Land Buddhism founded; Taoism influences poetry. Lo-Yang, capital.

635 — Nestorian Christian mission in China.

645—675 — Sanskrit books translated by Hsuan Tsang and others.

715—756 — Emperor Ming, founded School of Letters.

c. 845 — Ch'an (Zen) founded in China.

868 — Earliest extant printed book.

907—959 — Period of Five Dynasties.

701—762 — Li Po, great philosophical poet; Chinese poet best-known to the West.

836—847 — *Twelve Classics* cut into stone.

932—953 — *Nine Classics* printed on paper from wooden blocks.

III. Third Millennium (A.D. 960—Present)

1. Sung Dynasty (A.D. 960—1279)

Age inferior to preceding in literary arts but greater in diffusion of learning. Capitals: Kai-feng and Hang-chow.

1069—1074 — Socialist philosophers institute reform (Wang An-Shih).

11th Century — Golden Age of Landscape Painting.

1130—1200 — Great philosopher Chu Hsi, *Nature of the Universe*; author of encyclopedias. Neo-Confucianism.

2. Later Dynasties (A.D. 1260—1912)

1260—1368 — Yuan Dynasty. Capital at Peking. Kubla Khan, a Buddhist and Confucian.

1223—1296 — Wang Ying-Ling, author of primer used for 600 years.

1275—1292 — Marco Polo's travels.

1368—1645 — Ming Dynasty. Growth of arts, poetry, literature, encyclopedias and the use of tobacco.

1644—1912 — Ching (Manchu) Dynasty. Adopted Confucianism and allowed it to petrify.

1912 — Chinese Republic founded.

1036—1101 — Su Tung-Po, essay on poetic philosophy.

1050—1100 — Huang Ting-Chien, poet and calligrapher.

APPENDIX TWO

Yoga Asanas and Pranayamas

Yoga Asanas are not exercises in the sense of practice done with quick movements and a measure of strain involved. *Asana* simply means posture. In yoga, the word posture means a position that grants steadiness and comfort.

Symptoms of old age, such as wrinkles and poor complexion, are caused by poor circulation of the blood, thus leaving a lot of toxins and other waste matter in various parts of the body. Once the blood circulation is enriched, however, the foreign matter is washed out and eliminated, giving the body a younger look and feel.

As the yoga postures (asanas) and breathing exercises (pranayamas) are practiced, it will come to pass that the practitioner will benefit in three ways. First, he will develop a sound physical body which can cure itself of any ailment. Second, because of good health and complete alertness, he will be happier and able to benefit his family, occupation and surroundings. Finally, because he has united his physical being with his meditative mind, he will be able to tread the path of renunciation where he can seek oneness with all (and God).

What are the symptoms of good health? They include: real hunger, good digestion, sound sleep, perfect functioning of various organs of the body, proper pulsation, limited temperature, timely elimination of feces, urine and perspiration (within proper limits), interest in doing one's duties, happiness of the mind etcetera.

All these are proper functions of the body that daily practice of the asanas will grant. The major characteristic about the asanas is that they are done in a relaxed, unstraining manner. This differs from Western exercises, after a session of which a person is sweating, tired and has lost all energy to use for anything else. The asanas use little energy; in fact, they increase energy, making them more beneficial to everyone all the way around.

In Western terminology a person who is physically fit has a strong build with bulging muscles. In yogic terms a person who is physically fit has his nervous and endocrinal systems and organs working at par, and in addition to this, the mind is relaxed and free from any stress. The reason all these bodily systems are affected by yoga is because each asana massages a particular organ or nerve (whatever the case may be), making it larger and healthier. Along with the massage, the pranayama breathing enriches the area of the body that the asana has pinpointed.

The following photos will illustrate some popular asanas that the reader can try on his own. I must caution here that they must be performed slowly and comfortably. Do not strain. Yogis aim to be free from bodily and psychological stress; this can only be accomplished when the practitioner is in a relaxed, peaceful state. Each asana affects a certain part of the body, and I will illustrate this point with the respective asana.

POINTS OF INTEREST

TIME:
Yoga should be done either in the morning right after rising or in the evening before retiring. In both cases, the stomach should be close to empty. If the body is stiff, a brisk walk outdoors can remedy this. Beginners often find that they are more flexible in the evenings.

PLACE:
Asanas should be practiced in an airy room devoid of any disturbance. The ground should be level with no uneven surfaces.

DRESS:
Dress should be a bare minimum to allow the body to breathe. No restrictive clothing should be worn.

BATHING:
As a general rule, it is better to shower before an asana session. If you perspire in practice (beginners often will), then a shower can be taken twenty minutes after the session, *not before*. A cold or lukewarm water bath is most beneficial. An oil bath should be taken at least once a week for health, but *never before* an asana session.

THE ASANAS

1

ASANA:
Head Stand (Sirshasana, in Sanskrit)

TECHNIQUE:
Kneel, lock the fingers and create an angle on the floor with forearms by placing them on the floor in front of you. Place the crown of the head on the floor, close to the locked fingers, so that the fingers and forearms can support the head. Slowly lift the trunk, bringing it perpendicular to the ground. To do this, you must raise the knees and bring the toes near the head. When the trunk is raised you will feel that the toes and legs can be lifted off the ground without any jumping or jerking.

After feeling this out for a couple of sessions, slowly lift the toes and fold the legs so that the heels come close to the buttocks, with the soles facing up. Gently lift the thighs, bringing them to a horizontal position. Slowly straighten the thighs in line with the trunk of the body. Keep the spine erect. After a few days of this, extend the legs fully until you are erect. When coming down, perform the reverse of what has been mentioned.

TIME:
The beginner should perform each step on different days to allow the muscles time to prepare for the strain. In the first months of training the asana should be held for only ten seconds. Advancing yogis will perform this for twenty-five to thirty minutes.

BENEFITS:
This asana builds up a healthy brain. It influences the pineal, pituitary, thyroid and parathyroid glands. It will relieve most nervous ailments, especially the headache. This position benefits the body overall and helps relieve many diseases.

Photo model, George Taylor

2

ASANA:
Plow Pose (Halasana)

TECHNIQUE:
Lie flat on your back, keeping your hands alongside the body. Holding your breath, slowly raise the legs—without bending the knees, pressing the palms firmly against the ground. When the legs are at a 90-degree angle, raise the hips and the lower part of the neck and back, bringing the legs to a vertical position. Then, exhaling, slowly lower the legs over the head and touch the floor with the toes.

TIME:
Repeat three times for ten seconds. Can be held up to five minutes.

BENEFITS:
Elastic spine, healthy liver and spleen are assured. A healthy back is the key to youth. Helps in curing diabetes, neuralgia, indigestion and obesity.

3

ASANA:
Shoulder Stand (Sarvangasana)

TECHNIQUE:
Lie flat on your back, placing your hands alongside the body. Raise the legs up to 90 degrees. Then raise the trunk of the body to a vertical position also, until the chin presses against the chest. As you raise the trunk, simultaneously raise the forearms to support the back. The entire body from neck to toes should be as straight as possible. The back and neck should lie flat against the floor. To come down from the pose, gently lower the legs slightly over the head. Put your forearms on the floor behind the body. Drop the legs.

TIME:
One minute for beginners. Each week add a minute until you can hold for three.

BENEFITS:
Regulation of sex glands, poor blood circulation, seminal weakness and feminine disorders are cured by this pose. It helps in curing asthma, constipation, hernia and heart troubles.

CAUTION:
Keep the mouth closed. If saliva collects, do not swallow it, but dispose of it after posture is finished.

If you feel like sneezing, coughing or yawning while in the posture, come down immediately, before doing so.

Do not practice this pose if there is a disturbance in the organs of the head or if a headache or fever is present.

4

ASANA:
Head-to-knee Pose (Janusirshasana)

TECHNIQUE:
Sit on the floor with both legs stretched forward. Bend the left leg, placing the heel under the anus. Feel the pressure on the anus. Bend forward as much as possible, grasping the right toe with both hands.

TIME:
Sustain as long as you can. Repeat with left leg.

BENEFITS:
This pose helps to control sexual organs, evacuation of bowels and adds great flexibility to the leg and knee muscles.

5

ASANA:
Forward-Bending Pose (Jaschimothanasana)

TECHNIQUE:
Lie flat on your back, stretching the arms over the head and alongside the floor,

locking the thumbs. The upper arms should almost touch the ears. Stiffen the entire body, holding the breath, and slowly raise the arms, head and chest simultaneously, assuming a sitting position with the arms stretching over the head. See that the arms do not descend and that the legs do not jerk upward as you rise. After this, slowly bend forward exhaling, and hold on to the big toes with the index fingers and thumbs of the corresponding hands. Sustain the pose while breathing normally.

Little by little, bring the face down to the knees until the face is between them. The elbows should be bent, touching the floor.

TIME:
Maintain the pose for ten seconds at a time. In time, try to maintain the pose for a complete minute.

BENEFITS:
This is an excellent stretching pose. It tones every possible muscle in the body. It helps in curing hemorrhoids, constipation and diabetes.

6

ASANA:
Akarsha Shooting-arrow Pose (Akarsha Dhanurasana)

TECHNIQUE:
Sit on the floor, with legs stretching forward. Bend the left foot and catch hold of the right big toe with the left hand. Gently pull the left leg up until it touches the right ear. Use the right hand.

To "shoot-the-arrow," let go of left foot and allow it to hit the right foot.

7

ASANA:
Bound Head-to-knee Pose

TECHNIQUE:
Sit on the floor with the legs stretching forward. Bending the right knee, rest the right foot on the left thigh. Bring the right arm behind the back and grasp hold of the right big toe. Bend forward as much as possible, grasping the left big toe with the left hand and bringing the head to the knee.

TIME:
Hold as long as possible.

BENEFITS:
This pose improves general health, vigor and vitality. It helps to relieve chronic diseases of stomach, liver, spleen and intestines. It helps to remove hunch.

8

ASANA:
   Leg-to-head Pose (Ekapadhasirshasana)

TECHNIQUE:
   Sit with your legs stretching forward. Gently grasp the right foot, raising it over the head, and place it behind the head. Place the palms against each other in front of the chest. Come down and reverse the pose, pulling up the left leg.

VARIATION:
   Can be done lying on the floor.

CAUTION:
   Be sure not to force or strain the muscles or much damage will result.
   Take care in keeping the balance.

9

ASANA:
   Tortoise Pose (Koormasana)

TECHNIQUE:
   Sit with your legs stretching forward. Spread them as far as they will go. Lift the knees slightly. Bend the trunk forward, bringing the head to the floor. One by one, insert the arms under the corresponding knees. Stretch the arms backward, with the palms facing up (or down, for advanced). Slowly bend forward so that the chin rests on the floor.

10

ASANA:
    Backward Bend Pose (Poorna Supta Vajrasana)

TECHNIQUE:
    Sit on the floor. Assume a position with both hands resting on the thighs. Slowly bend backwards, arching the spine and bringing the crown to the floor.

TIME:
    Hold to one minute.

BENEFITS:
    Beneficial for kidney development and adds great flexibility to the back.

MEDITATIVE POSTURES

When selecting a posture for meditation, choose one that is comfortable and one in which you will be able to relax. The posture you choose will be both your friend and companion on the path of renunciation and thus should be one with which you can identify.

1

ASANA:
    Comfortable Pose (Sukhasana)

TECHNIQUE:
    Sit with the legs stretched forward. Comfortably cross the legs under the thighs. Keep the hands folded in front of the body.

BENEFITS:
    This pose is good for those who have little or no flexibility in the legs and thus could not adapt to other positions.

2

ASANA:
    Lotus Pose (Padmasana)

TECHNIQUE:
    Sit with both legs stretched forward. Rest the right foot on the left thigh with the sole turned up. Let the right knee touch the floor. Gently fold the left leg, bringing the left foot over the right thigh with the sole turned out. Both heels should be touching the

abdomen. Place the left hand between the heels with the palm turned up. Keep the head, neck and back in a straight line.

BENEFITS:
This pose is best suited for meditation and pranayama. It increases digestion, aids good appetite, helps in removing rheumatism and is an aid to strengthening the nerves of the legs and thighs.

3

ASANA:
Pelvic Pose (Vajrasana)

TECHNIQUE:
Kneel down on the floor, keeping the knees together. The entire length of the legs, from knee to toes, should be touching the ground. The heels should be apart and the toes should touch. Keep neck, trunk and head of body in a straight line.

CAUTION:
Keep the body completely relaxed and not tense.

BENEFITS:
This pose is useful in aiding digestion (if done after eating). It gives firmness and strength to the legs. It relieves gas, indigestion and dyspepsia.

PRANAYAMA

Pranayama means in translation "Control of the Prana," that is, the control of the life force or the "absolute energy." Prana is present everywhere and causes even the most subtle movements—for example, mental modification. By the regular practice of prana-yama, we are not only able to control the prana that flows within our being, but also the universal prana that flows everywhere. This is done through direct thought, the agent that directs prana.

POSTURE FOR PRANAYAMA:
The posture for the "breathing exercises" should be one where the head, neck and back are in line with each other and the hands rest on the lap or knees. I therefore suggest numbers two or three from the meditative poses.

TIME LIMIT ON PRANAYAMA EXERCISES:
For the beginner it should be under fifty breaths, never more than one hundred even for advanced pupils in one day.

CAUTION:
Pranayama is a very potent exercise and one should not attempt performance unless

the practitioner has adhered to the Yamas and Niyamas (see Yogic philosophy).

Because you are dealing with the heart, lungs and chest, strain must naturally be avoided.

1

PRANAYAMA:
Deep Breathing (Deergha Swansam)

TECHNIQUE:
Assume your meditative posture. Exhale slowly. Then inhale slowly. As you do so, expand the stomach and then the chestwell to allow a great amount of air to come in. Without holding your breath, exhale slowly. First drop the collarbone; then contract the chest and then the stomach, one section flowing into the other. The breath should be a continuous flow. Therefore, every inhalation should begin from the stomach and every exhalation from the top of the lungs.

2

PRANAYAMA:
Nerve Purification (Nadi Suddhi)

TECHNIQUE:
Assume a meditative pose. Calm the mind. Watch the breath for a minute with *complete* concentration. Place the index finger of the right hand between the eyebrows and close the left nostril with the second finger. Breathe in slowly and deeply through the right nostril, and when a full breath has been taken, close the right nostril, open the left nostril and breathe out through the left nostril. Now breathe in through the left nostril, close it, open the right nostril and exhale through it.

Time the intake of the air with the heart's beating. When inhaling, count four heart-beats, then hold for four beats and exhale with four beats (tempo of four-four-four). To slow the heart and calm the nervous system, breathe in slowly to slow the heartbeat down. To increase the heartbeat, breathe more rapidly.

TIME:
At the beginning, 25 cycles; more advanced pupils can increase up to 100.

BENEFITS:
Develops lightness of the body, alertness of the mind, sound sleep, and calm of body, mind and temperament.

3

PRANAYAMA:
Cooling Breath (Sitali)

TECHNIQUE:
Fold the tongue lengthwise like a tube. Project the tip of the tongue outside the mouth. Draw the air in through the tube, with a hissing sound. Fill the lungs to their limit. Draw the tongue in, close the mouth and retain the air as long as possible. Exhale slowly through the nose. This finishes one round.

TIME:
Do up to three rounds.

BENEFITS:
Cools off the body. It helps to remove heat, thirst, hunger and sleep.

APPENDIX THREE

I. Chronology of Zen and Ch'an Masters

This chart conforms to the Japanese version. The Japanese consider their Zen a direct descendant from the Chinese Ch'an introduced into China by Bodhidharma. I present it for the purpose of documentation.

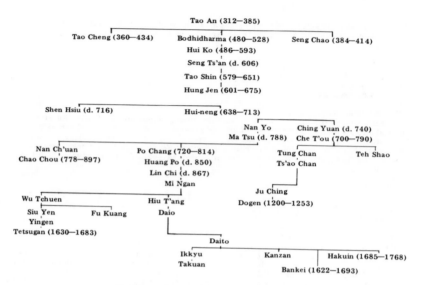

II. Chronology of Ch'an and Zen Masters

This chart conforms to the Chinese version. According to Chinese specialists, (1) Bodhidharma had no link between the 4th- and 5th-Century successors; (2) Bodhidharma's line tapers off after Shen Hsiu. The two schools of Zen thought (sudden awakening through wisdom called Prajnaparamita, and seated meditation called Lanka) come together after Hui-neng.

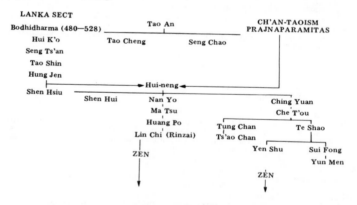

APPENDIX FOUR

A Guide to the Zen Meditative Technique

As seen in Chapter Nine, meditation can be a reflective state in which the meditator is trying to gain insight or wisdom about himself and the universe. This meditation can be considered of secondary importance when comparing it to the Zen meditative technique (see Chapter Five for the theory of Zen philosophy).

The Zen technique centers around the experience called "kensho" or seeing into one's own true nature. This can be approached in different ways depending on the school of Zen to which one adheres.

The student of Soto Zen will follow a strict style of meditation (as outlined in Chapter Nine) and wait for Self Nature to shine forth. For the student of Rinzai Zen, the koan is the main tool.

KOAN MEDITATION IN RINZAI ZEN

To start off this meditation, the Zen master (roshi) gives his student a starting koan on which to meditate. The student is required to treasure the koan in his heart and is to bear in mind the conduct of the patriarchs in their daily activities. He must squarely face the koan he has been given, studying it faithfully and working at it wholeheartedly. He will then pass beyond time. He will not be swayed by any external circumstances. His mind will be calm and composed and like a wall of iron. If this type of concentration is built up continuously over one year, two years, three years, *insight* into one's true nature will take place.

The realm which is revealed to us after we get this first glimpse into our Self Nature is called Dharmakaya in Sanskrit, or Hosshin in Japanese.

With the aid of our first koan we attain our first glimpse into the Hosshin. To remain in this place of peace and ultimately to go beyond it, we study many koans known as Dharmakaya koans, or in Japanese, Hosshin koans.

Now that we see our own True Nature, if we stop here we will never attain the experience the patriarchs have when they enter the marvelous realm of differentiation. To save ourselves from this misfortune, it is necessary to pass through many intricate koans having to do with this topic of differentiation. The Zen term for these complex interlockings of differentiation is "kikan." The koans which aid us in this are called Kikan koans.

With the help of Kikan koans we release ourselves from the bonds that hold us fast, and allow the spirit to return to the freedom of the open fields.

We must make our way through the mass of complex interlockings that make up the realm of differentiation, and enter into the sanctuary of the patriarchs. To accomplish this, we must retrain ourselves by concentration on our koans over and over again.

When the power of kensho is weak, we cannot be at peace with ourselves and cannot attain ultimate oneness.

The next type of koan we study are the Gonsen koans. Gonsen in translation means "the study and translation of words." Gonsen koans are the words and phrases that the patriarchs have said. They are complex and difficult to understand. Now that we have succeeded in entering the Hosshin, and in making our way through the interlockings of differentiation, we must devote our time and effort to penetrating the innermost meaning of words and patriarchal phrases.

After we understand the words we graduate to the Nanto koans. Nanto means "difficult to pass through," so we can see that the Nanto koans are those koans which are difficult to pass beyond. Even though we have seen into our Self Nature, moved through the multifold interlockings of Kikan koans and learned the meaning of the words of the patriarchs that are difficult to understand, to our regret we find that the dwelling place of the patriarchs is still as far away as the distant sunset. When we look at the bright red sphere it seems higher and higher; when we enter it, it seems deeper and deeper. This is the place called Nanto. Not until we penetrate the Nanto koans one by one can we be called true Zenists.

After we break through the unbreakable (the Nanto koans), we are almost at the summit of our formal Zen training. Even though we have penetrated many realms of experience, including the realm that is "difficult to pass through," the patriarchs want us to make a still deeper study of the doctrines of our sect. If this is the case we have to take up the Tozan Goi, or the "Five Ranks" devised by Tozan Ryokan Renji. These are often called the Goi koans.

The first rank is the "Apparent within the Real." This denotes the rank of the absolute, the rank in which one experiences the Tao (see Chapter One) and enters into the principle. The student will not enter this realm but break into it. It is said, "The empty sky vanishes and the iron mountain crumbles."

If the disciple remains in this rank of the "Apparent within the Real," his judgment will always be vacillating and his views prejudiced. Therefore, the disciple of superior capacity invariably leads his daily life in the rank of "Ever-Changing Differentiation." All the wonderful things about him and before his eyes—the old and young, the trees, grass and plants, halls and pavilions, mountains and rivers, verandahs and corridors—he regards as his own original, true and pure aspect. It is like looking into a still pond and seeing his face in it. This is known in Buddhist terminology as the Jeweled-mirror Samadhi, or that experience when all around you becomes you.

The third rank is when the disciple "Seeks Bodhi (wisdom) above, and saves Sentient Beings below." This is the so-called "coming-from within the going-to, and going-to within the coming-from." At this rank the disciple is more than a master, he is a Bodhisattva.

The fourth rank is when the Bodhisattva turns the "Dharma-wheel of the nonduality of brightness and darkness." He stands in the midst of the filth of the world, his head and body are covered with its dust. He is like a fire-blooming lotus that, on encountering the flames, becomes still brighter in color and pure golden fragrance.

Still, he must not think that this is the last state when his actions can affect if not cure the state of mankind. For there is one more rank: "Unity Attained."

When the disciple has completed the Five Ranks, it does not mean his study of formal Zen has come to an end, for the Zen way stretches endlessly, and there are no tarrying places on it. The Gates of Satori are manifold.

To aid the reader on his studies of Rinzai Zen, I would like to give a few examples of koans on each step so that the reader may try studying on his own. This is no substitute for a real teacher, but it is a start whereby one may discover if this path is for him. You must remember to select a quiet place for meditation, perform breathing exercises of your choice in order to calm the body and select a meditative posture that is right for you.

EXAMPLES OF HOSSHIN KOANS

A monk asked Kassan Osho: "What is the Dharmakaya?"
"The Dharmakaya is without form," Kassan answered.

* * *

When Ummon was asked, "What is the pure Dharmakaya?" he replied: "The flowering hedge surrounding the privy."

* * *

Jun Osho's verse on the Dharmakaya was this:

"When the cows of Eshu are well fed with grain,
The horses of Ekishu have full stomachs."

SOME EXAMPLES OF KIKAN KOANS

A monk asked Master Joshu: "What is the meaning of Bodhidharma's coming from the West?"
"The cypress tree in the garden," Joshu replied.

* * *

Three times the Master Chu called to his attendants, and three times the attendants answered him. The Master said: "I always used to think that I was beholden to you, but all along it was really you who were beholden to me."

* * *

A student asked Master Hakuin: "What is Zen?"
He replied: "Zen is nothing but he who asks what Zen is!"

SOME EXAMPLES OF GONSEN KOANS

A monk asked Master Joshu: "What is Joshu?"
The master told him: "East gate, west gate, south gate, north gate."

* * *

One day Chosha went for a ramble in the mountains. On his return to the monastery, the head monk said to him:
"Chosha, where have you been?"
"I have come from a ramble in the mountains."
"Where did you go, Chosha?" the head monk inquired.
"Going, I followed the fragrant grasses; returning, I pursued the falling blossoms."
"How very springlike the feeling!" exclaimed the head monk.
"Still better is the dripping of autumn dew from the full-blown lotus flowers," returned Chosha.
The master told him: "I am grateful to you for your answer."

* * *

A monk asked Fuketsu: "Speech and silence tend towards separation or concealment. How shall we proceed so as not to violate It?"
Fuketsu spoke with the following verse:

"I always remember Konan in the spring."

SOME EXAMPLES OF NANTO KOANS

Setcho wrote the following verse:

"Hearing, seeing, understanding, knowing—
Each of these is not separate.
For me, mountains and rivers

Do not appear in a mirror.
When the frosty heaven's moon has set
And midnight nears,
Whose shadow with mine
Will the clear pool reflect, cold?"

* * *

Goso Hoen Zenji said: "It is like a water buffalo's passing through a window-lattice. Its head, horns and four hoofs have all passed through. Why can't its tail pass through?"

* * *

Addressing the assembly at the end of the summer's sojourn, Suigan said: "My brothers, since the beginning of the summer I have done a lot of talking. Look, have I any eyebrows left?"
Hofuku said: "The robber has a coward's heart."
Chokei said: "Growing!"
Ummon said: "Mu (emptiness)!"

* * *

"Singing his poem, he rolls the bamboo blind high;
Having finished his nap, he parches the tea leaves dark."

OTHER FORMS OF MEDITATION

ONE-POINTING METHOD

The essential point of this meditation is to look at something actively, alertly and without the aid of any words. You pick an object to work with and look at it with the same structure as if you were feeling it, as if you were using your sense of touch to feel soft material. This object should be a natural symbol, a pebble, a twig, a seashell or an autumn leaf.

Let me give you an example: take a piece of velvet, stroke it, feel it. Do this for about thirty seconds. Now look at the object (in this case a piece of velvet) for the same amount of time you felt it. Really penetrate the object with your eye, "feeling" every facet of it. For most people there are two distinct feelings—of touch and of sight. When we use touch, our senses bring the stimulus directly to the mind where there is no confusion or doubt. In turn, when we use sight, the stimulus is translated into words and not into tangible "feelings." By practicing this concentration of staring at an object, we learn to feel with our sense of sight, and thus when we look out into the world we don't just "see" it but we "feel" it.

Once you have learned to concentrate by staring at an object (that is, when you can look at an object without thinking of anything else), the next step is to try to draw the image of your object into your body. This stage of the game is called by the yogis "fixed attention" and is an essential part of the One-Pointing Method.

When you learn to draw the object into your body (by continual practice), you may feel yourself grow lighter or heavier or feel as if currents of rather pleasant energy are flowing through your being. When you are this far, you have allowed the sense world to enter and pervade your being.

MEDITATION OF THE BUBBLE

In this meditation, picture yourself sitting quietly on the bottom of a clear lake. Picture each bubble that rises to the surface of the water as being a representative of each thought, feeling or perception. When you have a thought or time period or a feeling, observe it in this manner until the bubble is out of your range. Remember, a bubble is clear and you can see from one end to the other. In this way you can not only see your thoughts, but see "through" them.

This is a very structured meditation and can be called a meditation of the "inner way." What you are doing is meditating on the stream of your own consciousness while interfering with it as little as possible.

Do not be confused if the same bubble arises many times. If you just go on and treat each as a new consciousness, it will pass.

If you do not like the concept of bubbles, there is a variation of this method the Tibetan Buddhists use. They call it "the thoughts are logs method." In this meditation, picture yourself sitting on the bank of a broad river. From time to time, a log will float down the river, passing your seated figure. You follow the same procedure, using the logs instead of bubbles.

A HINAYANA MEDITATION

Hinayana meditation centers on the contemplation of self-generated rhythms. The goal is concentration; that is, doing only one thing at a time.

Lie on the floor with your hands resting on your chest or abdomen. Spread your fingers so that they are not touching each other and your hands are separate. "Feel" what is happening under your fingers; observe actively and observe with vigor. Do not translate the experience into words but into "feelings." Basically follow the same method as the One-Pointing Method, but contemplate with your fingertips instead of eyes and on your rhythm of movement rather than on a natural object.

THE LOTUS PETAL MEDITATION
The lotus is a symbol used in Eastern philosophy to represent the concept of everything being connected to every other thing. Where the Meditation of the Bubble was a method of the inner way, this meditation is structured so as to be a meditation of the "outer way."

A word, idea or an image is chosen by the meditator to be the center of the lotus flower. Words like love, peace, light, Tao, tree, eternity are good words for a beginner to start off with. Now that you have a center word, you form a lotus position and wait. In a few moments your first association of the word comes to you. You either understand the reason for the association or you don't. In either case you just think of the association for a couple of seconds and return to the center word for your next association. This is not a *free* association, because you are always returning to the center word for assistance.

This meditation, like the Bubble Meditation, often leads to great understanding about yourself and insights into your "inner life."

Start with ten minutes a day for two weeks, then go to a half hour a day for three weeks. At the end of this time you will know if this meditation suits you, and you will have a greater understanding of yourself.

MANTRA MEDITATION
The Mantra is the most widely used of the meditative techniques because of its simplicity and the small amount of time required for this style of meditation. The Mantra's basic purpose is to allow the mind to concentrate on only one thing at a time.

The Mantra is a chant that has two major purposes. The first concerns the content of the Mantra. The content helps you comprehend its known validity. Thus, if the Mantra, "All is One," is repeated enough, it will bring you closer to the knowledge of its truth. Also, by chanting "God is good," you will come to realize this state within your being.

The second purpose is to produce vibrations by the organization of various syllables. These vibrations will stimulate various organs of the body and thus stimulate their effectiveness.

By sitting in a lotus posture and repeating a chant, such as "Om, shanti, shanti, shanti, Om," you create a trance-like state and a rhythm of nature within your body. It is said that when this rhythm is mastered, the meditator has achieved oneness with the universe. To start this meditation, select a quiet place with dim lights. Start off chanting the Mantra for only 15 or 20 minutes and in time increase the chanting to 30 minutes. Any chant, such as "God is good," "God is One," "Nature is All" or simply "Om," will do for a start. (Refer to Meditation No. 50.)

"WHO AM I?" MEDITATION
In this meditation we ask the simple question, "Who am I?" and respond to each answer we come to realize. Thus, when we have placed ourselves in the proper position and chosen a quiet place, we relax and ask within ourselves, "Who am I?" and await what our minds will throw back at us.

If the answer to the question is your name, say to your mind, "No, that is a name I have given myself. Who is the *I* to whom I gave the name?"

If you respond, "I am the person who feels tired," say to your mind, "No, that is a sensation I feel. Who is the *I* who has this sensation?"

If your mind answers in a memory, such as "I am the person who once . . . ," say to your mind, "No, that is a memory. Who is the *I* who has that memory?"

If you picture an image of yourself, say to your mind, "No, that is an image of me. Who is the *I* who has this image?"

There is no rest in this meditation; it must be done with patience and perseverance. You must reject each answer until there are no more illusions to reject and you come to yourself, the *I*. This can take five to 50 years, but the satisfaction is beyond words.

UNSTRUCTURED MEDITATION
This meditation is of real importance, but it is the kind of thought that most of us experience through the course of our lives, especially if we have a lot on our minds. You choose an image, a concept, a relationship or a problem and think and "feel" it. You stay with the subject chosen, exploring its meaning, its nature and your feelings about it. This is not free association, for you are staying within the boundaries of a chosen topic. You are not daydreaming about the topic, but are actively exploring and working at it. Your purpose is to know, to comprehend the subject and your relation to it.

APPENDIX FIVE

Sermon at Benares

On seeing their old teacher approach, the five students agreed among themselves not to salute him or address him as master but to use his holy name only. "For," they said, "he has broken his vows and has abandoned holiness. He is no real student (bhikkhu) but Gotama, and Gotama has become a man who lives in abundance and indulges in the pleasures of worldliness."

But when the Buddha approached in a dignified manner, his fellow students involuntarily rose from their seats and greeted him in spite of their resolution. Still they called him by his name and addressed him as a friend instead of a teacher.

When they had thus received the Buddha, he said: "Do not call the Tathagata by his name nor address him as a friend, for he is the Buddha, the Enlightened One. The Buddha looks with a kind heart equally on all living beings, and they therefore call him 'Father.' To show disrespect to a father is wrong; to despise him, is wicked.

"The Tathagata does not seek salvation in austerities," the Buddha said, "but neither does he for that reason indulge in worldly pleasures, nor live in abundance. The Tathagata has found the middle path.

"There are two extremes, O bhikkhus, which the man who has given up the world ought not to follow—the habitual practice, on the one hand, of self-indulgence which is unworthy, vain and fit only for the worldly-minded—and the habitual practice, on the other hand, of self-mortification, which is painful, useless and unprofitable.

"Neither abstinence from fish or meat, nor going naked, nor shaving the head, nor wearing matted hair, nor dressing in a rough garment, nor covering oneself with dirt, nor sacrificing to a Fire-god, will cleanse one who is not free from delusions.

"Reading the *Vedas*, making offerings to priests or sacrifices to the gods, self-mortification by heat or cold, and many such penances performed for the sake of immortality, these do not cleanse the man who is not free from delusions.

"Anger, drunkenness, obstinacy, bigotry, deception, envy, self-praise, disparaging others, superciliousness and evil intentions constitute uncleanness; not verily the eating of meat.

"A middle path, O fellow students, avoiding the two extremes, has been discovered by me—a path which opens the eyes, and grants understanding, which leads to peace of mind, to the higher wisdom, to full enlightenment, and in time, to Nirvana!

"What is the middle path, O fellow students, avoiding these two extremes, discovered by the Tathagata—that path which opens the eyes, and grants understanding, which leads to peace of mind, to the higher wisdom, to full enlightenment, and in time, to Nirvana?"

The Buddha looked at them. "Let me teach you, my dear friends, the middle path, which keeps aloof from both extremes. By suffering, the emaciated devotee produces confusing and sickly thoughts in his mind. Mortification is not conducive even to worldly knowledge; how much less to a triumph over the senses! He who fills his lamp with water will not dispel the darkness, and he who tries to light a fire with rotten wood will fare terribly. And how can anyone be free from self by leading a wretched life, if he does not succeed in quenching the fires of lust, if he still hankers after either worldly or heavenly pleasures. But he in whom self has become extinct is free from lust; he will desire neither worldly nor heavenly pleasures, and the satisfaction of his natural wants will defile him. However, let him be moderate; let him eat and drink according to the needs of the body.

"Sensuality is enervating; the self-indulgent man is a slave to his passions, and pleasure-seeking is degrading and vulgar.

"But to satisfy the necessities of life is not evil. To keep the body in good health is a duty, for otherwise we shall not be able to trim the lamp of wisdom, and keep the mind ever so strong and clear. Water surrounds the lotus-flower, but does not wet its petals.

"This is the middle path, O friends of the Old Order, that keeps aloof from both extremes."

And the Blessed One spoke kindly to his once-fellow students, pitying them for their errors, and pointing out the uselessness of their endeavors, and the ice of ill-will that chilled their hearts melted away under the gentle warmth of their new master's persuasion.

Now the Buddha set the wheel of the most excellent law rolling, and he began to preach to the five students, opening to them the gate of immortality and showing them the bliss of Nirvana.

The Buddha said:

"The spokes of the wheel are the rules of pure conduct; justice is the uniformity of their length; wisdom is their tire; modesty and thoughtfulness are the hub in which the immovable axle of truth is fixed.

"He who recognizes the existence of suffering, its cause, its remedy and its cessation has learned the Four Noble Truths. He will walk in the right path.

"Right views will be the torch to light his way. Right aspirations will be his guide. Right speech will be his dwelling-place on the road. His gait will be straight, for it is right behavior. His refreshments will be the right way of earning his livelihood. Right efforts will be his steps, right thoughts his breath and right contemplation will give him the peace that follows in his footsteps.

"Now I will give you, O fellow students, the noble truth concerning suffering:

"Birth is attended with pain, decay is painful, disease is painful, death is painful. Union with the unpleasant is painful, painful is separation from the pleasant, and any craving that is unsatisfied, that too is painful. In brief, bodily conditions which spring from attachment are painful.

"This, then, O fellow students, is the noble truth concerning suffering."

The Buddha paused, then continued. "I will now give you, O bhikkhus, the noble truth concerning the origins of suffering:

"Suffering is the cause for the renewal of existence (reincarnation), accompanied by sensual delight, seeking satisfaction now here, now there, the craving for the gratification of the passions, the craving for a future life and the craving for happiness in this life.

"This, O bhikkhus, is the noble truth concerning the origins of suffering.

"Now this, my friends, is the noble truth concerning the destruction of suffering:

"Verily, it is the destruction, in which no passion remains, of this very thirst; it is the laying aside of, the being free from, the dwelling no longer upon this thirst.

"This, O bhikkhus, is the noble truth concerning the destruction of suffering.

"Now this, O friends, is the noble truth concerning the way which leads to the destruction of sorrow. Verily! it is this noble eightfold path; that is:

"Right views, right aspirations, right speech, right behavior, right livelihood, right effort, right thoughts and right contemplation.

"This, then, O friends, is the noble truth concerning the destruction of sorrow.

"By the practice of lovingkindness I have attained liberation of heart, and thus I am assured that I shall never return in the renewed births. I have even now attained Nirvana."

And when the Buddha had thus set the royal chariot wheel of truth rolling onward, a rapture thrilled through all the universe.

The devas left their heavenly abodes to listen to the sweetness of the truth. The saints who had parted from life crowded around the great teacher to receive the glad tidings. Even the animals of the earth felt the bliss that rested upon the words of the Buddha. All the creatures of the host of sentient beings, gods, men and the beasts, hearing the message of deliverance, received and understood it in their own language.

(The author wishes to thank Master Kuzure Kudo for his help in this translation of one of Buddhism's greatest pieces.)

Notes

[1] From the original Chinese text of the *Shih Chi* or *Records of the Historian* by Ssu-ma Ch'ien (145?—89? B.C.).

[2] Lau, D.C., *Tao-Te-Ching* (Penguin Books, 1967), pp. 45-46.

[3] Lewis, John, *The Religions of the World Made Simple* (New York: Doubleday & Company, Inc., 1958), p. 56.

[4] Wood, Ernest, *The Zen Dictionary* (New York: Philosophical Library, 1957), p. 47.

[5] Haines, *Karate's History and Tradition* (Tokyo: Tuttle Company, 1954), p. 83.

[6] Suzuki, D.T., *Essentials of Zen Buddhism* (New York: E.P. Dutton and Company, Inc., 1962), p. 253.

[7] Lu Ku'an Yu, *Zen and Zen Teachings: Second Series* (New York: Shambala, 1973), p. 71.

[8] Bernard, Theos, *Heaven Lies Within* (London, 1956), pp. 67-68.

[9] Evans-Wentz, *Tibetan Yoga and Secret Doctrines* (Oxford University Press, 1974), p. 118.

[10] Hoyland, John, "Song of Tukaram," in *An Indian Peasant Mystic* (London: Allenson & Co., 1932), p. 54.

Bibliography

Attar, Faridud-din. *The Conversation of the Birds.* Berkeley: Shanibala, 1971.

Bernard, Theos. *Heaven Lies Within.* London, 1956.

Chai, Ch'u and Chai, Winberg. *I-Ching.* New York: Bantam Books, 1964.

Chang, C.C. *The Practice of Zen.* New York: Perennial Library, 1959.

Ch'en, Kenneth. *Buddhism in China.* Princeton University Press, 1964.

Evans-Wentz. *Tibetan Yoga and Secret Doctrines.* Oxford University Press, 1974.

Feng, Gia-fu. *Chuang Tzu: Inner Chapters.* New York: Vintage Press, 1974.

Gaer, Joseph. *How the Great Religions Began.* New York: New American Library, 1963.

Gaer, Joseph. *What the Great Religions Believe.* New York: New American Library, 1929.

Haines. *Karate's History and Tradition.* Tokyo: Tuttle Company, 1954.

Hanh, Thich What. *Zen Keys.* New York: Anchor, 1974.

Hoyland, John S. "Song of Tukaram" from *An Indian Peasant Mystic.* London: Allenson & Company, 1932.

Humphreys, Christmas. *The Wisdom of Buddhism.* New York: Harper Colophon Books, 1960.

Iyen, Gar. *Light on Yoga.* New York: Schocken Books, 1966.

Kubose, Regnery. *Zen Koans.* New York: Regnery Books, 1974.

Lau, D.C., trans. *Tao-te-ching.* Penguin Books, 1967.

LeShan, Lawrence. *How To Meditate.* New York: Bantam Books, 1975.

Lewis, John. *The Religions of the World Made Simple.* New York: Doubleday & Company, Inc., 1958.

Ling, T.O. *A Dictionary of Buddhism.* New York: Charles Scribner's Sons, 1972.

Lu Ku'an Yu. *Zen and Zen Teachings: Second Series.* New York: Shambala, 1973.

McCartney, James. *Yoga: The Key to Life*. New York: E.P. Dutton and Company, Inc., 1969.

Miura. *The Zen Koan*. New York: Harcourt, Brace and World, Inc., 1968.

Raju, P.T. *The Philosophical Traditions of India*. Great Britain: University of Pittsburgh Press, 1971.

Ramacharaka, Yogi. *Philosophies and Religions of India*. Chicago: The Yogi Publication Society, 1930.

Reps, Paul. *Zen Flesh, Zen Bones*. New York: Anchor Books, 1968.

Ross, Nancy W. *The World of Zen*. New York: Vintage Press, 1972.

Smart, Niniak. *The Religious Experience of Mankind*. New York: Charles Scribner's Sons, 1969.

Smith, Huston. *Religions of Man*. Harper and Row, 1958.

Stryk, Lucien, and Ikemoto, Takashi, Eds. *Zen Poems, Prayers, Sermons, Anecdotes and Interviews*. New York: Anchor Books, Inc., 1963.

Suzuki, D.T. *Essentials of Zen Buddhism*. New York: E.P. Dutton and Company, Inc., 1962.

Suzuki, D.T. *Zen Buddhism*. New York: Anchor Books, 1972.

Trawick, Bucknerb. *World Literature, Vol. 1*. New York: Barnes and Noble Books, a division of Harper and Row, 1953.

Watson, Burton. *Chuang-tse: Basic Writings*. New York: Columbia Press, 1964.

Weigeil, James. *Mythology for the Modern Reader*. Lincoln, Nebraska: Centennial, 1974.

Wood, Ernest. *Yoga Wisdom*. New York: Philosophical Library, 1970.

Wood, Ernest. *The Zen Dictionary*. New York: Philosophical Library, 1957.

Yohannah, John. *A Treasury of Asian Literature*. New York: New American Library, 1956.

Yutang, Lin. *The Wisdom of China and India*. New York: The Modern Library, 1942.

Glossary

ADHIDHARMA — There are three divisions in the Pali canon; this is one of them. See *Tripitaka.*

AGAMA SUTRA — A collection of Buddhist Scriptures that were originally taken from the Sanskrit language. Today these Scriptures exist only in Chinese.

AMIDA — Japanese name for the ideal Buddha. In Sanskrit it is expressed as Amitayus or Amitabha, the Buddha of eternal life and boundless light (in Chinese, Amit'o Fa).

AMIDA SUTRA — The Smaller Eternal Life Scripture (in literal translation).

ANANDA — Cousin of the Buddha. He also served as his personal bodyguard and friend. He is also called Channah, which means sincerity and faithfulness.

ANGO — A traditional retreat for Buddhist monks. It is popularly used in the summer months.

ARHAT — One who has reached Nirvana. In Mahayana Buddhism it refers to one who is striving for enlightenment (personal), as compared to the Bodhisattva, who strives for enlightenment for all beings.

AVALOKITESVARA — A Bodhisattva of compassion (Kannon in Japanese; Kuan-yin in Chinese).

AVATAMSAKA SUTRAS — Basic texts for the Kegon Buddhist sect. These Scriptures have had great influence on the thought of Zen Buddhism. They stress the Buddhahood of all sentient beings, the identity of Samsara and Nirvana, and the theory of all Bodhisattvas as being full of compassion.

BELL STAFF — A staff with a bell affixed to its top. Used in Zen meditation and Buddhist ritual.

BHAKTI — Sanskrit word for devotion. Also a form of yoga that stresses the dualistic worshiping of God as separate from the individual, not within him.

BODHI — Buddhist term for wisdom or enlightenment. The Buddha received his enlightenment under the Bodhi tree.

BODHIDHARMA — Indian Buddhist monk who introduced Zen meditation to the Shaolin (Sil-lum) temple in A.D. 520.

BODHISATTVA — A man who has received his enlightenment but instead of dwelling in Nirvana chooses to remain on the earth, reincarnation after reincarnation, until all men have reached Nirvana. Also refers to a true seeker or one who is to become a Buddha.

BUDDHA — Translates as "One Who is Awake."

CH'AN — Chinese word for Zen. Founded in China by Bodhidharma.

CH'I — An intrinsic life force that is stored in the tantien (located three inches below the navel). It can either flow through the body (called Jun Ch'i), as in Acupuncture, or outside the body, as the force that makes an individual unique.

CHUANG-TSE — A book of Chinese philosophy written by a man bearing the same name, Chuang-tse (370—319 B.C.?). It is part of Taoism, stressing the mystical aspects of the universe.

CHUNG YUNG — One of the four books of Confucian literature. Called by its popular name, *The Doctrine of the Mean.*

CRAVAKA — One who seeks to overcome within himself the three poisons: greed, ignorance and anger.

DANA — To give or to share. One of the six principles of the Paramitas.

DHARMA — The Doctrine. It is the truth of Buddhism as declared by the Buddha. The truth itself.

DHARMA KAYA — See Tri Kaya.

DHYANA — Meditation as in contrast to Prajna or Wisdom. Dhyana is one of the branches of Yogic Wisdom (7th step) and one of the six Paramitas.

DIAMOND SUTRA — Part of the *Prajna Paramita Sutras*. A major text in the Mahayana Zen sect. It stresses the principle of Sunyata (emptiness).

DOKUSAN — Formal, individual instruction given to a shisho (student) by a Roshi (master).

ENLIGHTENMENT — Awakening of the True Self. Nirvana or Satori.

FIVE PRECEPTS — Called Sila. Buddhist morality (one of the six Paramitas). The Five Precepts are to abstain from killing, stealing, adultery, lying and intoxication.

FIVE RELATIONSHIPS — Confucian doctrine. In order of importance, the relationships of father to son, older brother to younger brother, husband to his wife, elder to younger, ruler to his people.

FORM — That which constitutes the appearance of an object. Necessary for an object to exist (Hsuang, in Japanese).

GASSO — or Gassho. A bow performed by placing both hands together, fingers pointing towards the sky and fingers set apart. Bow from the waist. Also, any gesture of respect.

GAUTAMA, GOTAMA — (Sanskrit and Pali, respectively). The family name of the Buddha. His first name was Siddhartha (563—483 B.C.). He was born in Kapila-vastu. His parents were King Suddhodhana and Queen Maya. First trying, then abandoning asceticism, Gotama adopted a middle path, attaining enlightenment and founding Buddhism. He lived to age eighty.

GRDHRAKUTA — Translates as "Vulture's Peak." The Buddha gave many sermons on this mountain.

HINAYANA — Translates as "Smaller (hin) Vehicle (yana)." The name given to the Theravada Buddhists by the Mahayana Buddhists. One of the two major schools of Buddhism, Hinayana stresses individual enlightenment devoid of any spiritual guide. It uses only the Pali canons (*Tripitaka*).

I-CHING — *Book of Changes*. Originally a book of great wisdom, today it has come to be used for divination. It is made up of 64 six-line oracles called hexagrams; these hold great wisdom and the secrets of the universe.

IDEOGRAPH — Chinese character. Originally a form of picture writing.

JI — Kegon Buddhists use this Japanese word to represent "individuality," or "form." It is contrasted to Ri or "void."

JU JITSU, or JU JUTSU, or JIU JUTSU — Translates as "the yielding art." A type of unarmed combat used by the Samurai or soldier of Japan (up until 1873). Zen was a major part of his training.

KALPA — Sanskrit word meaning "a long period of time." It is sometimes illustrated by the time it would take a rock, 40 miles square, to be worn to nothingness if every three years an angel landed and brushed it with the sleeve of its dress.

KARMA — The law of cause and effect. All conditions and states of existence are the direct result of previous actions, and thus present actions determine future events. Karma is also a system of yoga that stresses work over devotion or wisdom.

KARUNA — Translates as "Compassion." In Buddhist Philosophy, Karuna and Prajna (wisdom) go hand in hand, for compassion without wisdom may be misdirected, and wisdom without compassion can result in total isolation.

KENDO — The art of swordsmanship whereby awareness, discipline and self-mastery are placed above winning or killing.

KEN JUTSU — Swordsmanship with the intent to kill, using either a wakizashi (short sword) or a katana (long sword).

KOAN — Stories or problems given by Zen Roshis. They are meant to break the logical barrier of thought and allow the mind to reach enlightenment.

KOKUSHI — In China and Japan a kokushi is a National Teacher, a tutor to the Emperor and a religious and philosophical advisor to the whole nation.

KSANTI — Patience. One of the six Paramitas.

KUFU — Meditation that stresses the unification of the mind, spirit and body. The koan is a great aid to the kufu process.

KWAN-YIN — See Avalokitesvara.

LI — In Confucianism and Neo-Confucianism this term has meant four separate things. The first meaning is that of ritual or ceremony. Second, it means precepts that are laid down for a man to follow (i.e., Confucian maxims and anecdotes). Third, it is a personal ritual in which the individual is subjected to self-betterment. The forth definition was established by philosopher Chu Hsi, who defined Li as the form that makes things what they are. Contrasted to the Li is the Ch'i or the personality.

LI CHI — Book of Ceremonies and Rites. A major Confucian text.

LO-YANG — Capital city of China during the founding of both Buddhism and Zen.

LUN YU — Analects. This is a Chinese classic composed of the original sayings of Confucius himself. This text was compiled by later followers.

MAHAYANA — Literally, "Greater Vehicle." It is the second of the two great schools of Buddhism, stressing the idea of the Bodhisattva and the reliance upon a god.

MANDALA — Graphs in Shingon Buddhism symbolizing two aspects of the universe: (1) its ideal or potential entity, (2) its vitality or dynamic manifestation.

MANJUSRI — The Bodhisattva of wisdom.

MEAN — Confucian doctrine. It is often called the "Way that is Constantly in the Middle." It is the way between life's extremes. It prevents excess and checks depravity before it occurs. Its teachings are found in the Chung Yung (Doctrine of the Mean).

MEDITATION — Central to all Oriental Philosophy in one way or another. It is not used to deaden, but to awaken the mind to the truth of life.

MENG-TSE SHU — The Book of Mencius. Written by a follower of Confucius who stressed that man is good and that this goodness can affect others who have allowed the evils of society to affect them.

MIND — When capitalized, it refers to the Absolute, the Ultimate Reality.

MONDO — Zen questions and answers. Conversation in Zen. Similar to koan but in this case the answer is given. You must meditate on how it was arrived at. In the koan you must come up with the answer.

NAGARJUNA — Indian Buddhist philosopher of the 2nd Century A.D. He founded the Madhyamika school of Buddhism, which stresses the doctrine of Sunyata (emptiness).

NEMBUTSU — The calling of the name "Amida." This is a major practice of the Amida Buddhist sect. If performed correctly, it is a unique form of meditation.

NIRMANA KAYA — See Tri Kaya.

NIRVANA — Nirvana is often misunderstood to be mindless bliss or annihilation of the personality. It is neither of these. Instead, it is a state of awareness, complete oneness. It is the mind of the Enlightened One. Nirvana is the state of being subsequent to the annihilation of Samsara and identification with the Ultimate Reality.

NIYAMA — Second limb of the Yogic Tree of Enlightenment; ten things which must be avoided in order to stay on the correct path.

NYOI — Translates as "the mind wishes." A stick used by Zen masters for many purposes, including rapping dull students.

PA KUA — Translates as "Eight Diagrams." The term used to explain the original three-line trigrams that are used to make the hexagrams of the *I-Ching*.

PARAMITAS — A term used in Mahayana Philosophy to denote the six qualities or virtues that lead to enlightenment. They are: Dana (sharing), Sila (precepts), Ksanti (patience), Virya (perseverance), Dhyana (meditation) and Prajna (wisdom).

PARINIRVANA — Complete Nirvana. A term also used to denote physical death.

PATRIARCHS — Fathers of Buddhism. Each sect or school has its own lineage traceable back to the Buddha. Bodhidharma is considered the first patriarch of Zen.

PHILOSOPHY — Taking long-range, detached views of certain immediate problems. The love, study and pursuit of wisdom or knowledge of things and their causes, either theoretical or practical.

PRAJNA — Wisdom. The essence of the teachings of Zen. Also one of the six Paramitas.

PURE LAND — A Buddhist sect which originated in China. Scripture: *Sukhavativyuka (Great Eternal Life) Sutra*, stressing the realization of Amida and the description of the Pure Land (heaven/paradise, after Nirvana).

RI — Translates as the "abstract" or the "whole." It corresponds to Sunyata (emptiness) and the void.

SAKYAMUNI — "Sage of the Shakya Clan," a name often given to the Buddha.

SAMADHI — The state of highest concentration in meditation.

SAMANTABHADRA — Bodhisattva of Love. Fugen in Japanese and P'u Hsien in Chinese.

SAMBHOGA KAYA — See Tri Kaya.

SAMSARA — The Wheel of Rebirth. The cycle of birth after birth.

SANZEN — Formal Zen meditation at a temple.

SARIRA — Gem-like stone found in a person's bones after cremation.

SATORI — Japanese term for the enlightenment experience.

SENSEI — Japanese term for a teacher.

SHANTI — Sanskrit word for "peace." Used in reciting yogic chants. (Should be chanted three times, i.e., "Om, shanti, shanti, shanti.")

SHIH CHING — *Book of History*. One of the Five Confucian Classics.

SHU CHING — *Book of Poetry*. One of the Five Confucian Classics. The poems are supposedly written by Confucius himself.

SILA — See Five Precepts.

SUKHAVATIVYUKA — *Great Eternal Life Sutra*. The basic sutra of the Pure Land sect.

SUMI-E — Japanese brush painting.

SUNYATA — Emptiness. See Void.

SUPERIOR MAN — The ideal man as Confucius saw him. All Confucian Classics and texts stress how one may become such.

SUTRA — Term for the Scriptures.

TA HSUEH — The Great Learning. One of the Four Books of Confucian literature. It expresses the idea of the Superior Man.

TAO — (Do, in Japanese). Translates as the "Way," "Great Principle." The Tao gives substance to the universe and patterns the laws of life.

TAO-TE-CHING — The major text of Taoism. It was once called the Lao-tse after its mythical founder Lao-tse ("Old Philosopher"). The text is made up of 81 poems expressing the ideal of the Tao and how a man might pattern himself after it by living a simple, passive and reflective life.

TATHAGATA — A word meaning "Suchness," "Thus Come," or "As It Is." It is also another name for Buddha.

TE — Translates as "Power." To the Taoist, power meant the way the Tao can manifest itself (i.e., either by magic, philosophy or mysticism). To the Confucian, power meant the power within each and every one of us to do what is to be done.

TENDAI — A Buddhist sect introduced into China by Dengyo Daishi in 805 A.D. Teachings are based on the Lotus Sutra, which stresses the universality of Buddha-nature and its attainment.

TEN DIRECTIONS — The Universe. The ten directions are: north, south, east, west, northeast, northwest, southeast, southwest, above and below. Commonly known as the Ten Quarters.

THERAVADA — Translates as the "Teachings of the Elders." Same as Hinayana.

THIRD AGE — See Three Ages.

THREE AGES — A term used to describe the three periods of Buddhist Philosophy. First age, Buddhism is truly taught and practiced; second age, formality and ritual and third age, Buddhism declines and even the formality is abandoned.

THREE POISONS — They are the three things that prevent the Satori and Nirvana experience. They are: greed, ignorance and anger.

TIPITAKA — A canon of Buddhist Scripture written in the Pali language. These texts are used mainly by the Hinayana sect. In literal translation, Tipitaka means Three Baskets. They are: the Vinaya (rules of governing monks); Sutta or Sutra (words of the Buddha); Abhidamma (condensed doctrine abstracted from the Suttas).

TRANSMIGRATION — The leaving of the spiritual essence of one at death to another at birth. Commonly called rebirth. In Buddhism it refers to Samsara.

TRANSMISSION — The passing of one Dharma to another, from mind-to-mind. In a temple when the transmission takes place, the person receiving the honor is given control of the temple and the two signs of authority, a bowl and a robe.

TRI KAYA — Translates as the "Three Bodies." Mahayanist view showing the relation of the Ultimate Reality to man. The three bodies are: Dharma Kaya (the formless, colorless, timeless Absolute); Sambhoga Kaya (the ideal expression of the Absolute, e.g., Amida Buddha); Nirmana Kaya (the actual living expression of the Absolute, e.g., Gotama Buddha).

TRIPITAKA — Sanskrit for Tipitaka.

VOID — Sunyata, or Emptiness. Not used to mean "now there is nothing, where before there was something." Rather, it is emptiness in the sense that reality has no fixed doctrines but is a continuous flux.

VULTURE'S PEAK — See Grdhrakuta.

WAY — See Tao. In Buddhism it meant the "Way of the Universe."

WISE MAN — In Confucianism it refers to a man who is one step below a Superior Man and one step above the ordinary man. A man who is on the path.

YAMA — In Yoga, the second branch of the "Yogic Tree," comprised of Ten Rules that a student of yoga must follow to be on the right path; things he must do.

YANG — In Chinese Philosophy it refers to the positive elements of the universe.

YARROW STICKS — Traditionally there were 42 of them. When cast they drew out a hexagram to be consulted in the *I-Ching*. The Yarrow Sticks were first asked a question, then they were thrown. The answer to the question is found in the hexagram. Today Chinese bronze coins or pennies are used.

YIN — In Chinese Philosophy it refers to the negative elements of the universe.

YOGA — A Sanskrit word meaning "to yoke." Yoga's aim is to unite the mind and the body in order to attain Nirvana. There are various methods which a student can use as an aid toward Nirvana. Physical exercises, meditation, devotion, work, knowledge, sound, sex and symbols are just a few.

ZAZEN — Sitting Zen meditation.

ZEN — A branch of Buddhist Philosophy brought from India to China in 520 A.D. There are three major sects to Zen: Rinzai, Soto and Obaku. Rinzai stresses abrupt awakening and makes use of the koan; Soto emphasizes sitting meditation and the submergence of one's self in his own personal, unique koan; and Obaku teaches gradual means to enlightenment.

ZENDO — Meditation hall.

Index

About the Author

George Richard Parulski, Jr., was born in Rochester, New York. He attended Bishop Kearney and St. John Fisher College to study philosophy and biology. He now teaches Oriental philosophy at St. John Fisher College. To further his knowledge of philosophy, he lived for three years at the Eisho-ji, a Zen temple in Corning, New York, where he received his enlightenment under Roshi Kazure Kudo (died in 1974). Parulski's articles have appeared in *Unity Magazine*, *Rosicrucian's Digest*, *Personal Growth*, *New Thought*, *Vegetarian Times*, *Orion Magazine* and *East/West Journal*.

Apart from philosophy, he finds time to write fantasy and science fiction. In the field of fantasy he has written *Adventures of Tim Amulet*. In science fiction his story, "October's Children," won the 1974 Quasar award for excellence in SF writing.

About the Illustrator

Carolyn Iachetta Parulski was born in Rochester, New York, in 1952. She studied at the Rochester Institute of Technology. In 1971, she won the Scholastic Award for art excellence for a water transparency. Her sumi-e illustrations have won kudos. Among her illustrated books is the fantasy classic, *The Adventures of Tim Amulet*, authored by her husband.